EXPERIMENTING WITH CALLIGRAPHY

For those at No. 2 and J.

KLMN

PEACOCKS AND LILIES FOR INSTANCE

OPQRS

TUVW

XYZ

JOHN RUSKIN

Margaret Daubney

Experimenting with Calligraphy

A Masterclass

B. T. Batsford, London

AUTHOR'S NOTE

Particular thanks are due to those friends who lent pieces of work for illustration; to Gillian for her contribution to the book projects; and especially to Munni for all her support and encouragement and for the extraordinary hard work and creative energy which she put into the production of this book.

First published in Great Britain in 1995
by B. T. Batsford Limited
4 Fitzhardinge Street
London W1H 0AH

ISBN 0 7134 7657 5

A Cataloguing Record for this book is available from the British Library

Conceived, produced and designed by
SAVITRI BOOKS LTD
115J Cleveland Street
London W1P 5PN

for the Publishers
B. T. BATSFORD LTD

Art direction and design by Mrinalini Srivastava
Edited by Caroline Taggart
Photography by Matthew Chattle
Typeset in Cheltenham Book Condensed by Type Technique, London W1
Colour origination produced by Mandarin Offset, Hong Kong
Printed and bound in Spain by International Graphic Service, Toledo

ACKNOWLEDGEMENTS
The illustrations on pages 48 and 64 are reproduced by kind permission of The Board of Trustees of the Victoria and Albert Museum. The picture on page 27 is reproduced by permission of The Trustees of the British Library.

CONTENTS

PROJECTS

INTRODUCTION

For centuries calligraphy, the art of beautiful writing, was an important craft affecting the political, religious and intellectual lives of people. Today it has become an art form which, because of its versatility, has a wide and growing appeal. It is still concerned with fine writing, but it is now a much more varied and exciting craft and a deeper and more satisfying art than that definition suggests.

Some of the traditional methods haven't been bettered and are still used by the contemporary calligrapher, but we have tools, materials, ideas and purposes which were unknown to the medieval scribe. Today we can use calligraphy to write a label or a formal presentation address, to write a card, a book or a dramatic interpretation of a poem. Our horizons are so wide that it is sometimes difficult to know where to begin and how to progress. One of the aims of this book is to help you to use what you learn so that you can move on, using your own ideas and interests.

If you are a beginner, your first concern is to acquire the techniques. You will learn to handle the tools and materials and to understand the principles of good letter form. If you follow the exercises and experiments in this book carefully, these skills will develop gradually. Don't expect great things to happen quickly. If you learn to play the piano you will be able to play a simple tune in a week or two, but it may take ten years of study to turn you into a musician. So it is with calligraphy.

The best way to learn a skill is to look, think, understand and practise. I first studied calligraphy by joining an adult education evening class where I was given a printed worksheet of alphabets and instructed to copy them. It took me most of the first term to learn one alphabet, then I moved on to a new one and instantly forgot the first. I'd learned to look and to practise, but not to think or to understand.

The formal letter studies in this book have been presented so that you will be able to understand and remember what you are writing. You may find it disconcerting that there are no 'A–Z' alphabets to copy, but if you read the explanations you will see that this way of learning letters is logical, straightforward and actually much easier than trying to copy 26 shapes.

Complete explanations of all the exercises and experiments are given in the text; many of them are illustrated, though some give just an idea of what your experiments will look like. If you want to be a better calligrapher you must do a lot of writing and there are plenty of ideas for writing practice given in the experiments.

After a very short time you will have enough knowledge and skill to be able to make real things, to write out a favourite poem, make a birthday card or just address a parcel dramatically. The projects in this book are Real Things made for Real People and have been chosen to suggest ways of using your skills and ideas as they develop. Remember that calligraphy is a personal thing: your writing and your work won't look like mine. Your interpretation is important, so bring in your own ideas, be brave and experiment.

'But I haven't any imagination,' students regularly say to me. *Everyone* has imagination, you may simply have forgotten how to use yours. One of the aims of this book is to suggest some ways to revive your imagination, to encourage you to experiment so that you will be able to find and use new ideas. Formal calligraphic studies begin with rules, but these rules are much more flexible than you may think. Ultimately writing must be appropriate to its context, aesthetic to its maker and comfortable to produce, but you can only make such judgements if you understand what you are doing. The emphasis in this book is on looking, thinking, on being flexible and self-critical.

Creating and making a piece of calligraphic work is a very pleasurable activity. The rhythmic movement of a well-sharpened nib on a good piece of paper, the shine of wet black ink, the shapes and colours of letters growing on the page, the patterns and textures of a design as they fall into place are all part of the enjoyment of writing. You will also have the satisfaction of using your skills and your creativity.

Calligraphy is about patterns, shapes, colours, textures, making abstract pictures. It is also about words, ideas, interpretation, communication. It is visually pleasing, intellectually satisfying, practical, useful, sensual, emotional, personal. It can be frustrating, exhilarating and fun. It is much, much more than beautiful writing. I hope this book will help you to enjoy it as much as I do.

PENS, INK AND HOW TO BEGIN

Before you begin, your first concern is for where and how you sit to work. The more comfortable you are, the more you will be able to concentrate on producing good work. So how to achieve this relaxed and productive state?

The first point is to appreciate that you write not with your fingers but with your whole body, so all of you must be at ease. Your chair or stool should allow you to sit with a balanced posture and it must be the right height for your table or desk. You should sit upright but in comfort, so that your back can work and your arms can move. I remember when I was ten years old being told by my piano teacher that the piano was played with the feet. While I was wondering how to respond to this dangerous lunacy, he explained that if my feet were firmly and squarely on the ground, my body would be balanced above them and this balance would give me freedom of movement and strength and weight to my arms and back. He was quite right, and the principle works for calligraphers too.

The second point is that you need to be sitting in the right place, which means a well-lit space near to a good light source. If you are right-handed the light should come from your left, and vice versa for left-handers. Ideally it should come from a window and be supplemented by a lamp when necessary. The traditional artist's clear northern light is best of all. It is always easier on the eyes to work in daylight.

The third consideration is a drawing board. This can be a very large, and very expensive, professional draftsman's table, an adjustable drawing board which sits on a table, or an off-cut of blockboard from your local DIY store which you prop on your knee against the table edge. The nature of the board is not really important; what matters is that for most of your work with ink or paint you will need to work at an angle. Write flat on the table and gravity will defeat you. The ink will flow too quickly and will be very difficult to control. Write with too steep a board and the ink may not flow at all. My wooden drawing board is usually raised to an angle of about 25°. Experiment with yours at different angles and decide what is most comfortable for you.

The work station. The surface of the table has been covered with paper to protect it and the drawing board pushed back so that you can see the equipment clearly. As I am right-handed, the pens, ink and mixed paints which are in use are immediately to my left. I use brushes in my left hand to fill the pen held in my right. Other equipment such as pencils, penholders and tubes of gouache are stored in plastic containers to the right of the board. A ruler, scissors and an eraser are always readily to hand. The drawing board, padded to give a good working surface and raised to a comfortable angle, is moved to the edge of the table when in use.

Whatever kind of drawing board you are using, it should be firm and rigid enough to act as a support, but you should pad the working surface so that there is some response in it and to make it more comfortable to work on. Mine is padded with sheets of blotting paper and cartridge paper. You will also need a guard sheet to protect your work from the natural grease and oils in your hand. Some people like to tape a piece of paper across the lower part of their board, secured only at the outer edges of the board, so that the writing hand can rest on it while the work in progress slides up and down behind it. I find it more comfortable to have a piece of folded layout paper resting on my work and under my hand. It doesn't matter what method you use provided you have a barrier between your hand and your work.

The fourth, and perhaps most important, point is that your writing area should be organized for your convenience, so that you are able to reach the ink easily, your pencils (sharpened), ruler, paints, spare nibs are readily accessible and your writing hand is resting comfortably on the work in progress. Don't forget to move your paper up the board as your writing advances towards the bottom of the page and to move the paper to the left as you write along the line.

Once you have a comfortable place to sit, you need to consider your equipment. To begin a proper study of the craft of calligraphy you need pen, ink and paper.

We are all used to writing with pens which do the hard work for us. The modern fountain pen and the ballpoint are sophisticated instruments. The ink flows readily on to the paper and is easily controlled however awkward our grip, however heavy or light our pressure on the paper and however good or bad our handwriting.

If you haven't tried formal calligraphic writing before, it is a good idea to use a square-cut felt-tip or a calligraphic fountain pen for your first attempts. They are both easy to handle and will feel comfortable and familiar. However, you will soon realize that these complex modern tools have their limitations. The felt-tip quickly becomes soft, the colours are unsubtle and it is almost too easy to use; you will learn nothing of the movement, of the pace and rhythm which are essential to good calligraphic writing from it. Some fountain pens have soft

Opposite page. *A selection of basic calligraphic equipment. The top row, from left to right, shows 3 penholders, 2 Automatic pens and a Coit pen, a mapping pen, a calligraphic fountain pen, 2 broad-edged fibre-tip pens, a pencil, a carpenter's pencil, 2 brushes to be used to mix paint and to fill nibs, 2 wedge-shaped brushes to use as writing tools. Beside the penholders is an Arkansas stone on which steel nibs can be gently sharpened and a selection of steel nibs and reservoirs. An eraser and a pencil sharpener are useful. It is worth buying a 45 cm (18 in) ruler like the one to the left of the layout pad. On the pad are black and red ink sticks and an ink stone, watercolour paints, mixing dishes and, in the bowl, tubes of gouache and a bottle of non-waterproof ink. Below the pad is a straight edge for cutting against, a craft knife, geometry instruments, low adhesive tape, glues, scissors and a bottle of gum arabic.*

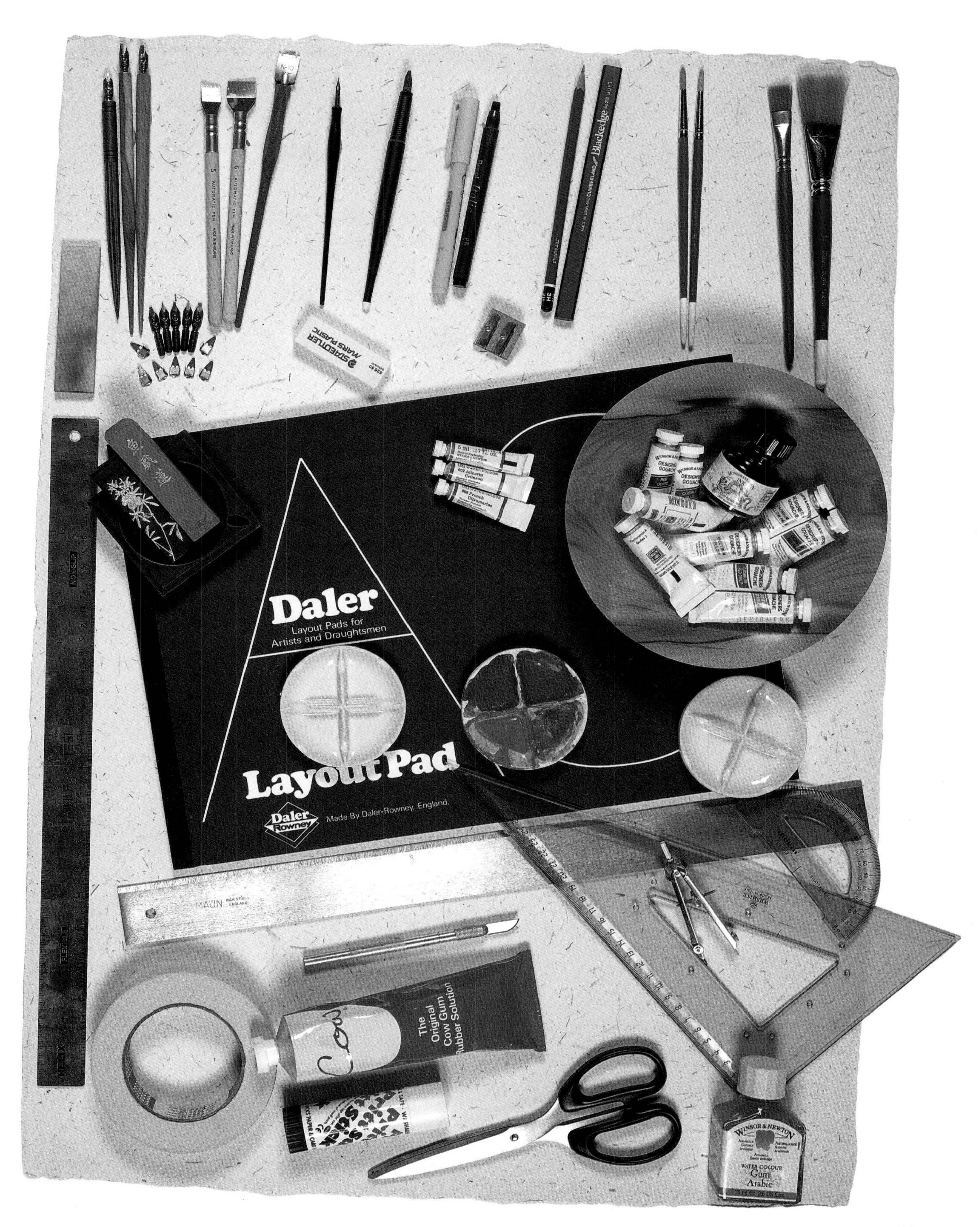
STAEDTLER
MARS PLASTIC
Blackedge
Daler
Layout Pads for
Artists and Draughtsmen
Layout Pad
Daler Rowney
Made By Daler-Rowney, England.
STAINLESS STEEL RULER
NON-SLIP
FLEXIBLE
HELIX
MAUN
The
Original
Cow Gum
Rubber Solution
Cow
WINSOR & NEWTON
WATER COLOUR
Gum
Arabic

nibs, some manufacturers offer only a narrow range of nib sizes and you will usually find that you are limited to the inks supplied with the pen.

So most calligraphers choose to use loose steel nibs which have to be set into a penholder and fitted with a reservoir. Such a pen is a much more primitive tool. It has to be held correctly, it has to make proper contact with the paper and the writer's touch is very important. It takes skill to make it work, but once mastered it is infinitely more versatile and flexible than any fountain pen.

If your art shop stocks more than one type of penholder, choose the one which feels most comfortable. You will need several penholders, a full range of square-cut nibs (oblique-cut if you are left-handed) and a few reservoirs.

Layout paper in A3 size (about 11½ in x 16½ in) pads is necessary for writing practice, drafts and rough work. Don't attempt to economize by buying a smaller pad – you will fall off the edge of your page as soon as you begin to experiment – and don't indulge yourself with better quality paper for your first trials – it may not do the job as well as layout paper.

Any non-waterproof black ink is suitable for calligraphy, but the different brands do have different consistencies and sometimes the same brand will vary from batch to batch. You may have to try two or three different varieties before you find one you like. The problem is solved if you make your own, which isn't as difficult as it sounds. You will need an ink stone and a Chinese ink stick. Place a few drops of distilled water on the stone, then gently rub the stick in the water in a circular movement until it thickens into ink. Because this ink is heavier than most bottled inks, it flows more slowly in the pen and many calligraphers find that this makes it easier to control. You can also make it as black as you need it to be. Stick ink has to be freshly ground each time you want to use it, but this is a very good way to begin the day's work and helps to concentrate the mind on the tasks ahead.

If you have some calligraphic experience and any of these suggestions is unfamiliar to you, it may be worth trying it out; anything which helps you to write a little more comfortably will eventually show in your work.

Opposite page. *Written in gouache on NOT watercolour paper with an Automatic pen. The colours merge because different pigments were fed into the pen at the same time. The line break-up was created partly by the speed of the writing and partly by the texture of the paper. Image size 230 x 190mm (9 x 7½ in).*

FIRST MARKS

Opposite page.

1. Fitting the nib.
The nib should be pushed well down into the space between the outside plastic or wooden shell of the pen and the inner metal spring. Make sure that the nib fits firmly and doesn't wobble.

2. Fitting the reservoir.
The wings of the reservoir slip on to the shoulders of the nib. If it is difficult to slip the reservoir on to the nib, ease the wings a little with your thumbnail. The metal is quite soft and will bend easily. If the reservoir is loose on the nib, squeeze the wings to tighten it. The tip of the reservoir must just rest against the nib. Again, you may need to bend the reservoir to make it fit.

3. Reservoir in position.
The reservoirs are here in position for writing. If your ink is flowing too freely, or not flowing well, a minor adjustment to the reservoir will sometimes solve the problem. To clean your nib each day, first remove the reservoir and then take the nib out of the penholder. Clean both nib and reservoir in warm water. Don't put your penholder in water as this will rust the inner metal spring.

4. Holding the pen; sitting correctly.
The pen is held loosely between the thumb and first finger and rests lightly on the second finger. Notice that a guard sheet is protecting the work from the hand resting on it. Try to sit upright and comfortably so that your writing arm can move freely.

Your final act of preparation is to put your pen together. This can be quite a tricky business if you've never done it before, but if you understand what you are doing and why, it should become easier. If you are a more experienced calligrapher and having trouble with your pen, these photographs and suggestions may shed light on your problem.

The nib should fit firmly in the penholder. If it wobbles, you haven't pushed it in far enough and your writing will wobble too. Then you must fit the reservoir carefully on to the nib to create a space to hold the ink. When you put your pen on to the paper to write, the tines of the nib ease and the ink flows down the slit to the edge of the nib and on to the page. If your reservoir is gripping the shoulders of the nib very tightly, the tines won't ease and the ink won't flow. If your reservoir is loose, it may fall off, usually into your bottle of ink. Don't be afraid to bend or squeeze the reservoir to make it do its job.

The tip of the reservoir should just touch the nib. If it doesn't, there is nothing to hold the ink in and it will fall in a blot on to your work. If the reservoir presses on the nib, the tines will be permanently splayed and the nib damaged.

As the reservoir is there to control the flow of the ink, it is best to fill your pen by dipping a brush into your ink and then painting the ink into the space created between the reservoir and the nib. If you dip your pen into the ink bottle, you will fill the reservoir but you will also have ink clinging to the top of the nib and the underside of the reservoir, and again that may drop and blot your work, or your shirt, or the carpet.

One last suggestion before we begin to use the pen: look closely at how it is held in the photographs. It sits lightly between the first finger and the thumb and rests on the second finger. It is held loosely because the fingers are supporting, rather than gripping, it. If you hold your pen lightly and close to the end of the holder, you will be able to feel the paper through the nib. So to the first experiment.

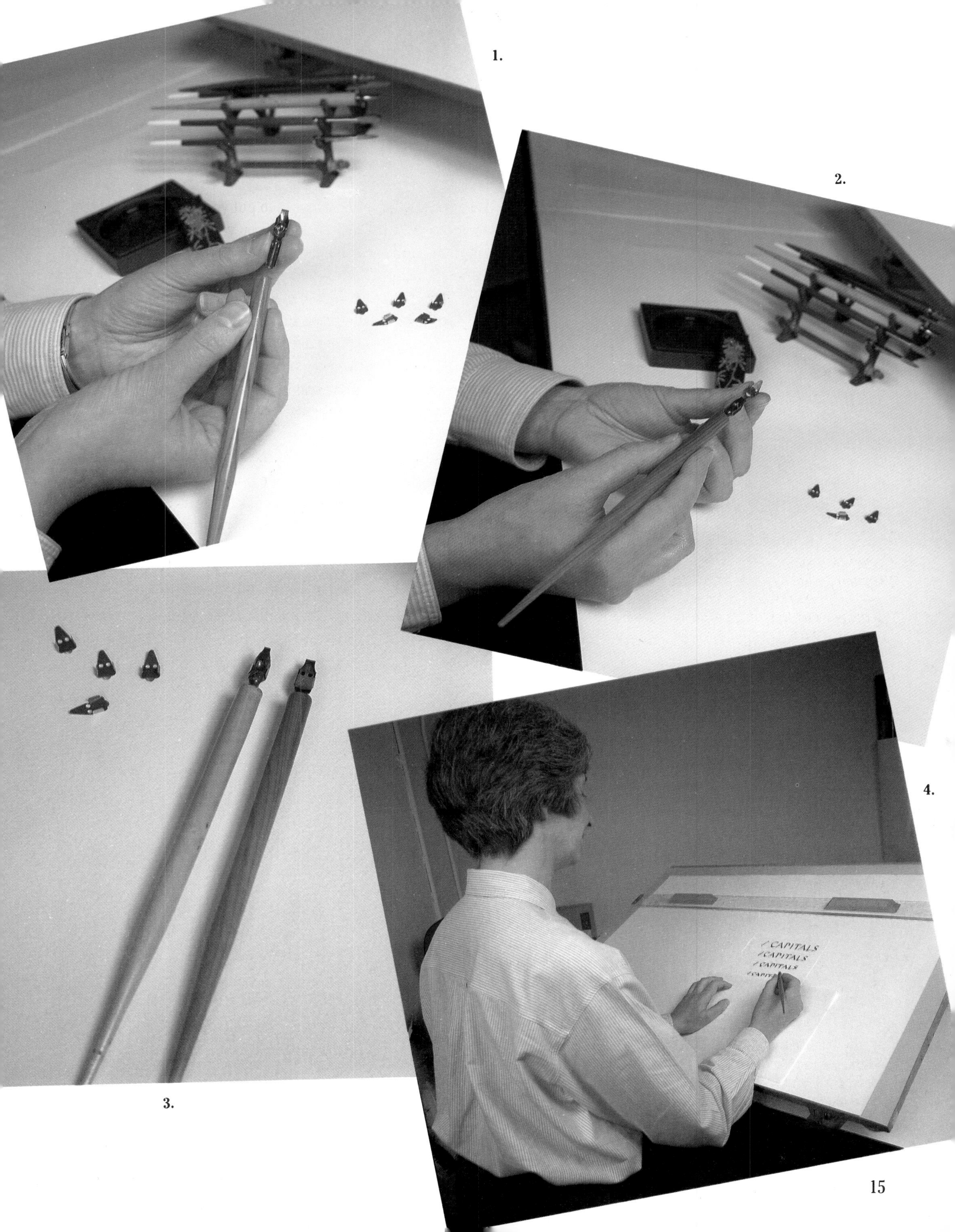

1.

2.

3.

4.

Put your pen together using your broadest square nib, fill the pen with ink and on a sheet of layout paper draw a series of straight lines from the top to the bottom of the page. Draw your lines as steadily as possible and press firmly enough to feel the paper through the nib. You will soon realize that working slowly with an even pressure and moving your arm rather than your fingers will produce a cleaner, stronger line. Take time to get the feel of the pen in your hand and on the page, and don't expect beautiful things to happen at once. Being able to drive a car doesn't mean that you can drive a lorry or ride a bicycle, and being able to write with a ballpoint pen doesn't mean that you can write with a dip pen. You are learning a new skill using an unfamiliar instrument.

If you have a calligraphic fountain pen, a square-cut felt-tip and/or a carpenter's pencil, try repeating the same lines with these. Hold each tool in the same way as you hold your dip pen, feel the differences as you draw your lines and look at the differences in the marks you are producing. A calligrapher can write with anything – I recently met one who was doing beautiful things with a piece of string – but it is important to choose an instrument that will make the right image for the task in hand. The bite of a steel nib on paper and the strong black line of good ink help to create marks which are appropriate for formal writing, but you should file away all the other ideas – they will have their uses later.

Experiment 1

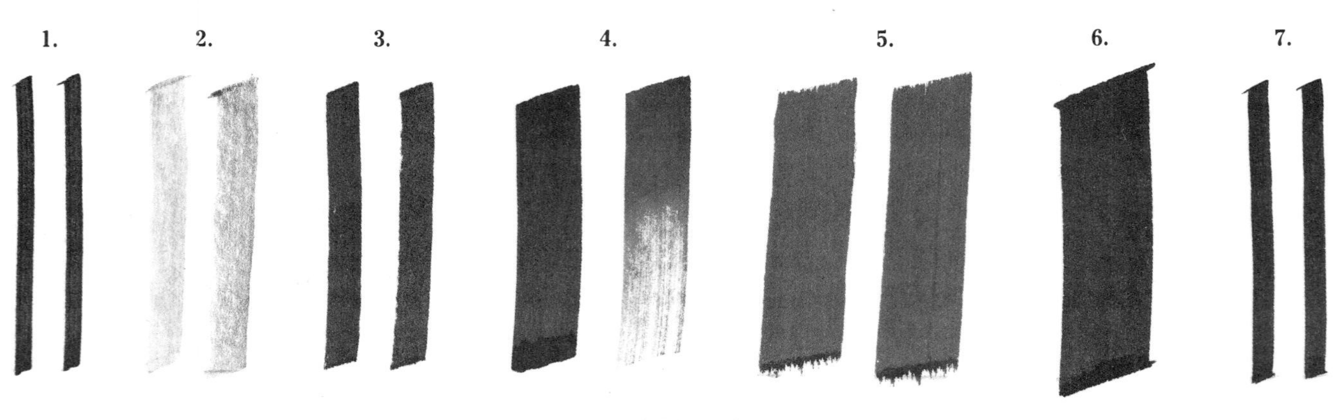

Left to right.
1. Calligraphic fountain pen
2. Carpenter's pencil
3. Broad-edged fibre-tip pen
4. Piece of balsa wood
5. Piece of wood veneer
6. Automatic pen
7. Rexel steel pen

Now return to your dip pen and copy the marks in Experiment 2. Continue to work at a steady pace; this rhythmic movement is an important part of formal writing. You will find that the same nib can produce a wide range of marks if you vary the angle between the edge of the nib and the line along which you are drawing. The characteristic thick and thin marks of calligraphic letters are created simply by holding the pen at a particular angle, so it is very important to be aware of exactly how you are holding your pen. Try Experiment 2 again and look at what you are doing with your pen as you do it.

Experiment 2

So far we have only worked in straight lines, but Experiment 3 moves on to curves. While you were trying out different pen angles in the last exercise you probably discovered that some marks were more comfortable to make than others. It is not easy to make a very thin line with the edge of the nib and it is harder to draw a horizontal line than a vertical one. As a general principle, it is easier to pull the pen than to push it.

Experiment 3

Begin by copying the first mark of Experiment 3, starting at the top of the stroke and curving down to the bottom. Now copy the same mark, but begin at the bottom and curve up to the top of the stroke. Your second stroke almost certainly felt more difficult because you were pushing the pen; it is also unlikely to look as good as the first stroke. This is why many of the letters of formal calligraphic alphabets are made up of two or more strokes. If the hand pulls the pen, which means that strokes move from top to bottom and from left to right, it has more control and makes a better mark.

Try the rest of Experiment 3 bearing this in mind and noting that you will need to change your pen angle quite frequently.

For Experiment 4 you will need plenty of paper. Still using the same large nib, take each of the marks in turn and, keeping the shape as accurately as you can, first reduce each one step by step until it is as small as you can make it, and then enlarge it as much as you can. Keep your arm relaxed and moving easily, and don't hurry.

Experiment 4

Earlier we showed that one size of nib can produce an endless variety of lines if the angle of the nib is altered. Now you can see that the same nib, held constantly at the same angle, can produce an endless range of sizes, each size having its own 'look'. Your smallest square will look very dense and black, your largest may be so lightweight that it is hardly recognizable as a square, but they both have the same form and were made with the same tool.

If you have worked carefully through these experiments, you will be using your pen with greater confidence and ease, you will have learned a great deal about what the broad-edged pen can do, about which marks come easily to you (and which don't), and about being comfortable while working. You will also, although you may not realize it, have learned a great deal about formal calligraphic writing.

A formal hand should be written steadily and rhythmically, the letters built up by a series of strokes enabling the pen to move in a comfortable and controlled manner. The choice of angle between the edge of the nib and the writing line must be an informed and deliberate decision, as must the choice of the form and weight of the letters, because all these will affect the 'look' of the writing.

Now you are ready to think about forming letters.

Experiment 4 (cont.)

BEGINNING TO WRITE

Above and pages 22–23. *These blocks of pattern were made using a selection of broad-edged coloured fibre-tip pens. Notice that different shapes are made according to the way in which the pen is held. The reproductions are real size.*

We usually think of a pattern as a purely decorative design repeated in an orderly and disciplined fashion. Most humans, whatever their cultural background and in whatever time they have lived or are living, seem to like patterns. We use pattern, and apparently always have done, in an enormous variety of contexts, the designs varying from the simple, and therefore easy to copy and imitate, to the complex and sophisticated designs of highly skilled eyes, hands and intellects. Patterns decorate the facades and walls of grand buildings, the floors and ceilings of cathedrals, the plates from which we eat our breakfast toast and the supermarket carrier bag; we put them on our walls and on our clothes, on our curtains and on our carpets. Consider the different patterns illustrated on pages 22–23.

Look at a Roman mosaic floor, a carefully laid brick path, an orderly and well-planned garden or a traditional patchwork quilt. These are all essentially useful, serving specific practical purposes, but their creators have taken the trouble to organize the materials decoratively, choosing colours and shapes and textures with great care.

We enjoy the ornamental qualities of pattern, the colour, form and exuberance of pure decoration, but we also like discipline and order, and that is one reason why patterns are so important to us. We can wonder at and admire the sophisticated artist's skills which created William Morris's wallpaper designs, but we are also comforted because each design is highly structured and contained; we feel that it is manageable, comprehensible. We like variety, but not too much of it.

And that is part of the reason why formal writing is so satisfying. It is disciplined and structured, but it also allows for great freedom when the skills are mastered. Like the Roman mosaic floor, medieval calligraphy was essentially useful, a means of communication in a largely illiterate world, but it was also treated as a decorative art in its own right.

Writing is about repetition – I have already emphasized the importance of using the pen rhythmically and evenly, and if you are writing a formal hand, your aim is to repeat the same letter shapes as accurately as you can – but it is also about variety, about devising your own rules and using writing to do what you want it to do. One of the discoveries you will make as you progress through the experiments in this book is that however carefully you follow instructions, your writing will come out looking like you. Even the most formal calligraphy is very personal.

Like the patchwork quilt, your letters can come in as many shapes, sizes, colours and textures as you wish, provided you understand what you are doing, and that your aim is to create a design, to make a pattern. In this group of exercises, you will be using the skills which you have already practised, but in a much more disciplined manner, turning marks into patterns.

Rule a series of pencil lines about 5cm (2in) apart across a page of layout paper and, again using your broadest nib, copy the patterns shown in Exercise 1, this time writing on the pencil lines. Be as accurate as you can. Note that these marks are of all shapes and sizes and that the pen has to be held at various different angles to produce them. Check that you are holding your nib at the right angle to make each mark, write steadily and remember to take your pen off the page and to make two strokes where necessary so that you are always pulling rather than pushing your nib.

Exercise 1

For Exercise 2, again rule pencil lines on which to write and copy the marks as accurately as possible. This time you are being asked to write with your pen held at a consistent angle and, as you can see, there is more uniformity and a better

sense of pattern in the marks you are making. The edge of your pen should be at an angle of about 30° to the writing line. This is how you will be holding your pen for the study of Foundational hand, which we will come to in the next section; it is worth spending some time getting used to the feel of your pen held this way and familiarizing yourself with the look of the shapes you are producing.

Exercise 2

Of course you will find inconsistencies in my examples and there will be inconsistencies in what you write. That is part of the nature of writing. What matters, as with so many calligraphic techniques, is that you understand what you are trying to do and constantly keep striving to achieve it.

If you now look back to Experiment 4 on pages 18–19, you will notice that the same basic shapes – a square, a curved line – were made to look very different according to their scale. The tiny square looked black and solid because so much of the white space had been squeezed out of it, whereas the largest square looked weak and loose because there was so much white space inside it. The proportion of black line to white space in your letters helps to determine the overall look of your writing, so making a considered decision about it is very important.

This is the next discipline to be imposed on your writing. Rule more pencil lines if you need to, take your pen and hold the nib at 90° to the line. Make four marks as shown in Exercise 3 as carefully as you can. These marks are measuring the width of the edge of your nib, because your first letters are to be four nib-widths high. Now take your ruler and draw another pencil line parallel to the first. These guidelines will give you the correct height for the letters you will be practising, but the lines must be drawn as accurately as possible if they are to be useful. Take your time and be patient.

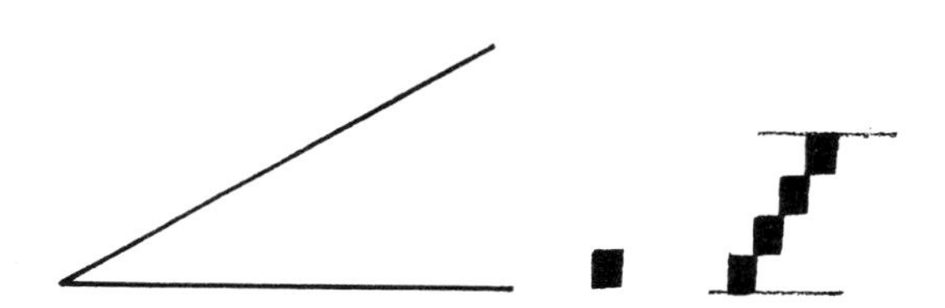

When you have some guidelines ruled, try the patterns in Exercise 3. As you can see, the discipline of working with a consistent pen angle and a uniform height makes the patterns more evident. As you work, keep checking that you are holding your pen at a 30° angle and that your marks are just touching both top and bottom guidelines.

Exercise 3

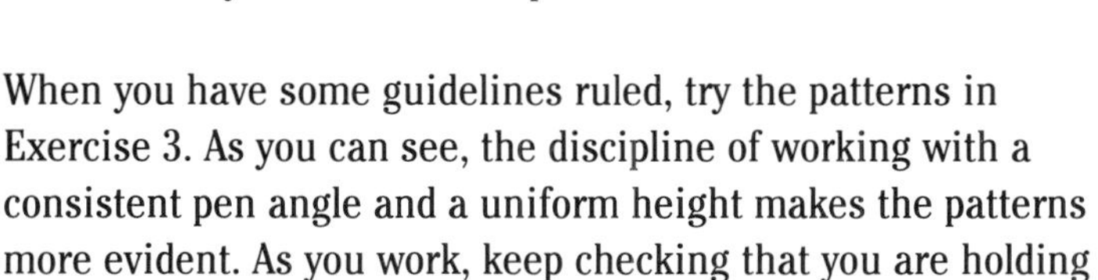

When you are ready to go on, work through Exercise 4. Look carefully at the way in which the shapes sit between the guidelines, sometimes but not always touching the lines; look at the white spaces between the marks and at the ways in which the marks begin and end.

If you have worked patiently through all the experiments so far, you will have some skill and understanding of formal calligraphy and I promise that your patience will be rewarded very soon. You may have been tempted to skip quickly to the first alphabet which you intended to copy, turning instantly into A Calligrapher, but if you have worked through the exercises you will realize that that would have been impossible. To learn a new skill requires practice, understanding and more practice, but it is worth the effort. You now know almost all you need to know to write a formal calligraphic hand.

All you have to do is put it all together.

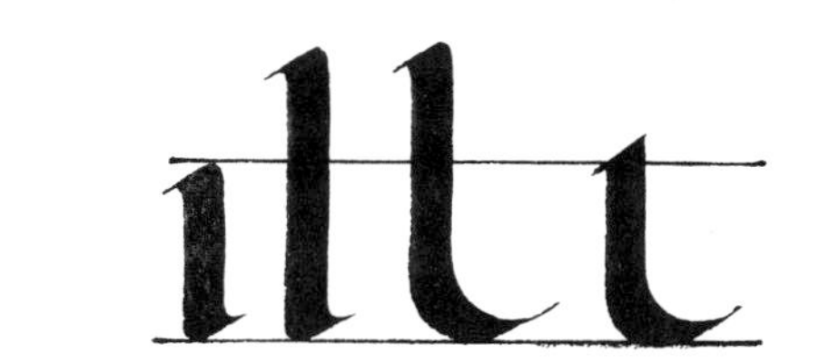

Exercise 4

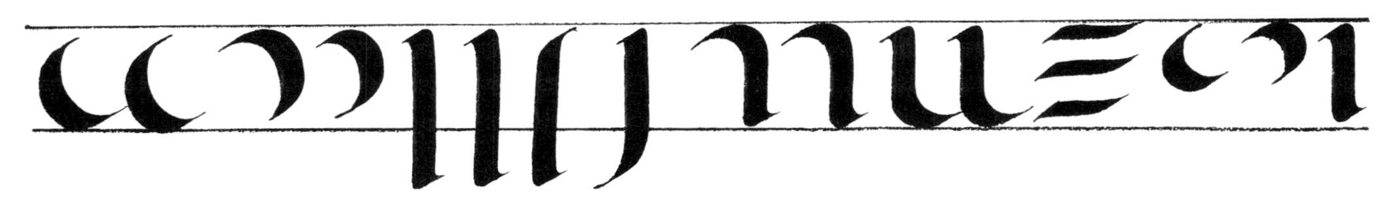

FOUNDATIONAL HAND – A STUDY

The Ramsey Psalter, now in the British Library in London, was written at the end of the tenth century in the southern half of England, and probably at Ramsey Abbey near Huntingdon. The language is Latin, the hand in which it is written an English Caroline minuscule, and the manuscript is an essential element in the development of twentieth-century calligraphy.

In nineteenth-century Victorian Britain, the tradition of calligraphy as a craft and as a decorative art, which had been weakening over a very long period, seemed to have been broken. A revival of interest began with William Morris and the Arts and Crafts Movement from about the 1860s. With the eye of both a printer and a calligrapher, Morris studied medieval manuscripts, produced decorated and illuminated manuscripts himself and used his researches in the work of the Kelmscott Press.

However, although we owe a lot to Morris's work, the re-establishment of a thriving calligraphic tradition, which has continued with increasing vigour through the twentieth century, has been due to the researches, writings and teachings of Edward Johnston.

Johnston came to London as a young man in 1897, met Sydney Cockerell, who had been Morris's secretary, and W.R. Lethaby, founder of the Central School of Arts and Crafts and also a friend of Morris. Johnston was encouraged by them to pursue his interest in manuscripts by studying in the British Museum. It was Cockerell who suggested that he should study the Ramsey Psalter, and it was on this manuscript that Johnston based his Foundational hand, a hand which he used in his own commission works but which he devised as a teaching hand to practise with his students.

The Ramsey Psalter has many of the qualities a calligrapher looks for in an historical model. Primarily, of course, it is real writing done by a real scribe for a real purpose and all these have influenced the character of the writing. The scribe's chief concerns were to use a style of writing which was appropriate to his task, which his eye, and presumably that of his superior, found pleasing and which his hand could produce comfortably.

Opposite page. *A page from the Ramsey Psalter. London, British Library, Harley Ms. 2904. Thought to have been written between 974 and 986 AD. Page size 330 x 250mm (13 x 9¾ in).*

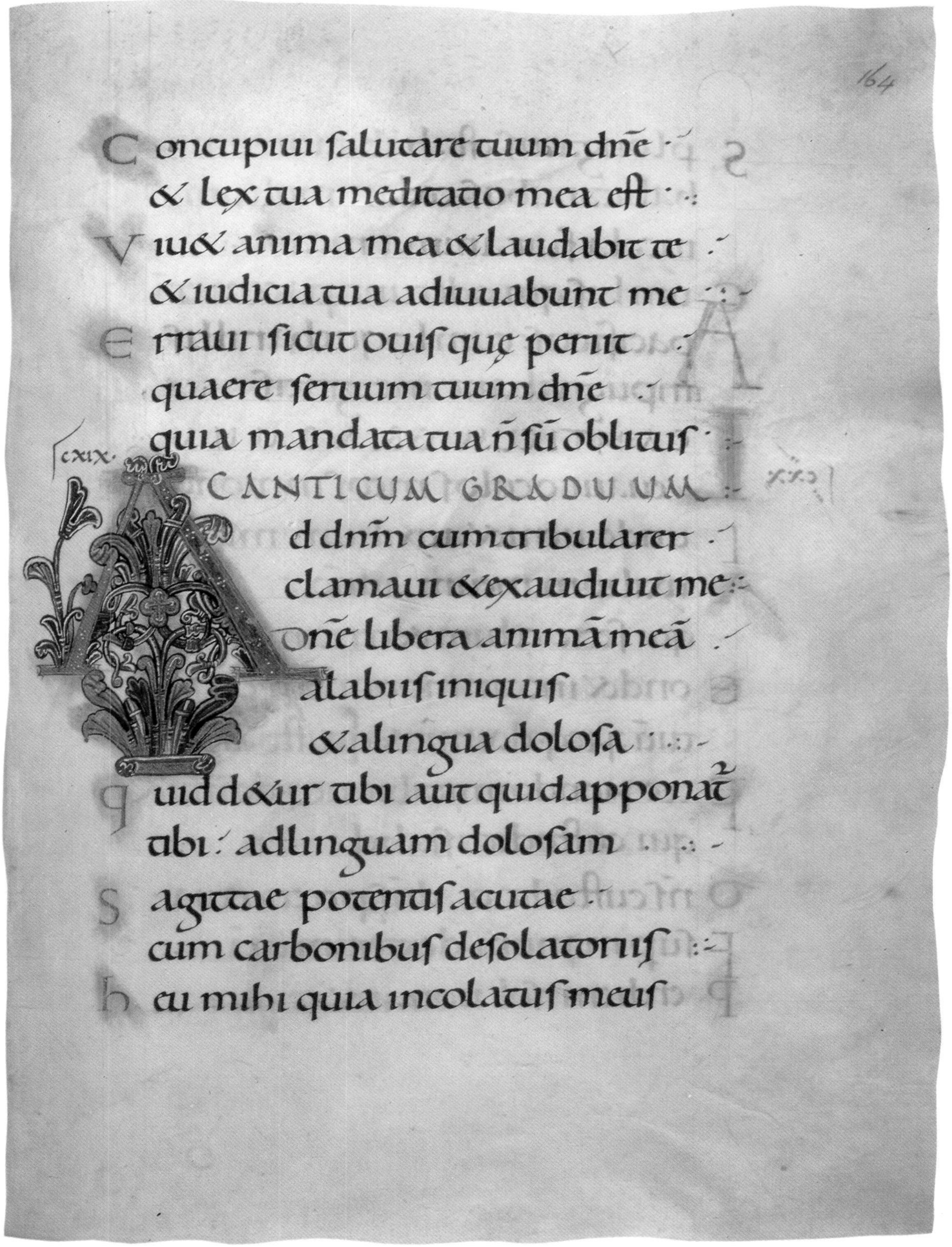

164

Concupiui salutare tuum dn̄e
& lex tua meditatio mea est
Viuę anima mea & laudabit te
& iudicia tua adiuuabunt me
Erraui sicut ouis quę periit
quaere seruum tuum dn̄e
quia mandata tua n̄ sū oblitus

CXIX. CANTICUM GRADUUM

Ad dn̄m cum tribularer
clamaui & exaudiuit me
Dn̄e libera animā meā
a labiis iniquis
& a lingua dolosa
Quid de&ur tibi aut quid apponatur
tibi ad linguam dolosam
Sagittae potentis acutae
cum carbonibus desolatoriis
Heu mihi quia incolatus meus

The writing is strong, quite large and easy to read; it doesn't have idiosyncrasies which might distract the reader from the content of what he is reading, or the contemporary calligrapher from the basic structure of the letters. It is also written with great vigour and control, suggesting that the scribe had both skill and confidence. When choosing a model for study, always choose one of the highest quality.

Because this is very skilful, real writing, it is regular and controlled, rhythmic and even, but not totally even. This is where your earlier experiments with patterns become useful.

If you look carefully at the extract from the Psalter you will see that certain marks are repeated, including some of the marks which you were practising in the last set of experiments. Try not to see letters or words, but look at the patterns which the writing is making on the page. This is always difficult because we have been trained from an early age to see words as information which must be read. However, this text is not only in Latin but in a Latin in which the scribe has used elisions to abbreviate his material, making some of the letter combinations even less familiar. But if you are still distracted by the words, try turning the text upside down to look at it – the patterns might become more evident.

When you followed the experiments with patterns in the last section, it is unlikely that you were able to repeat shapes exactly, although with practice and experience they would become increasingly regular and even. So it is with formal writing. The scribe must have a clear idea of the patterns, the marks, which are to be written and must try to repeat those ideas as accurately as possible.

If you look through the manuscript passage and pick out every letter 'a', you will see that they are not exactly the same as each other, but are very similar. Every time the scribe wrote an 'a' he had the same idea in his mind and hand; he was trying to repeat a pattern.

A printed reproduction can only give an idea of the extraordinary qualities of the writing; to see the real manuscript is an exhilarating experience. The writing is so vigorous and lively that it almost leaps off the page and there is an unnerving sense of contact with a craftsman who suddenly seems to be a very real person, even though he was working a thousand years ago.

Presumably Edward Johnston also felt this sense of communication. He studied the writing of the Psalter, and after making a few modifications and amendments used it to introduce the principles of formal writing to his students.

Johnston's influence as a researcher, teacher, designer and craftsman can hardly be exaggerated. His students, and their students, include many of the most important calligraphers and letterers of this century, and his handbook, ***Writing and Illuminating and Lettering***, published in 1906 and still in print, is seminal.

The influence of the scribe of the Ramsey Psalter has also been enormous. It was his writing which prompted Johnston to formalize his teaching and to devise the hand which has been a starting point for study for calligraphers ever since.

But we are now at the other end of the twentieth century and calligraphy has progressed, changed and moved on, so why do so many calligraphers still begin their studies with Foundational hand, particularly when a contemporary Foundational hand looks a little different from Edward Johnston's version? The important thing to appreciate is that the look of a formal hand may owe something to the taste and fashion of its time, but that the principles by which it is constructed and formed are timeless. If writing is to be alive and vigorous, it must be relevant and of its day.

It is pointless for us to try to reproduce the marks of the Ramsey Psalter scribe exactly. He was working a thousand years ago, using quill, vellum and ink made to the local recipe. Many modern scribes work with quills and vellum, some almost exclusively, and doubtless there are those who make ink to their own recipes, but most of us use paper and steel nibs and our marks inevitably have a different quality. Similarly Edward Johnston, who worked with quills and often on vellum, was writing in a different age and his work is marked by the tools he used and the tastes of his period. To study a formal calligraphic hand is not to copy or to imitate, but to understand the ideas, the principles and the patterns which make up the hand.

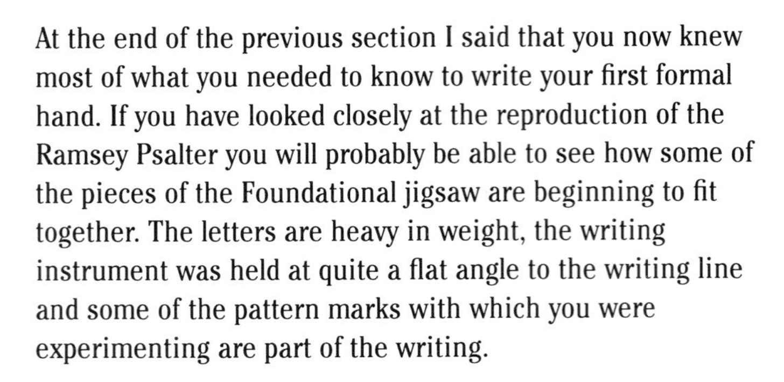

At the end of the previous section I said that you now knew most of what you needed to know to write your first formal hand. If you have looked closely at the reproduction of the Ramsey Psalter you will probably be able to see how some of the pieces of the Foundational jigsaw are beginning to fit together. The letters are heavy in weight, the writing instrument was held at quite a flat angle to the writing line and some of the pattern marks with which you were experimenting are part of the writing.

To write this version of the Foundational hand, you will once more need your broadest nib and plenty of pencil guidelines which are four nib-widths apart. The bodies of the letters are written between these guidelines, ascenders and descenders as in 'd' and 'p' rising above and dropping below, and the pen is held at an angle of 30° to the writing line. You are already familiar with the look and feel of letters made this way.

The third element in a formal hand is the basic letter shape – for this hand it is the circle. All the letters relate to the circle and are based on its dimensions. This is what gives the writing its pattern.

Holding the pen at 30° to the horizontal writing line, begin just below the upper pencil line and draw a half circle as in Exercise 1. If your pen angle is correct and your lines are four nib-widths apart, the curve which you draw will begin at its thinnest point, swell to a thick stroke and then diminish again just as you lift your pen. Take time to get this stroke right; make your mark slowly and steadily and really look at what you are doing on the page.

Exercise 1

This is the first basic mark of the Foundational hand and it is repeated in several different letters.

The second basic mark is a mirror image of the first. Put your pen on the paper just below the top pencil guideline, curve up to the line and round and down to the right, lifting your pen when you feel that you are beginning to push rather than pull.

The third basic mark is the straight line because this gives the pattern for the serifs. The serif is the mark which begins and ends a written stroke and it serves the practical purposes of getting the ink going at the beginning of a mark and tidying it up at the end.

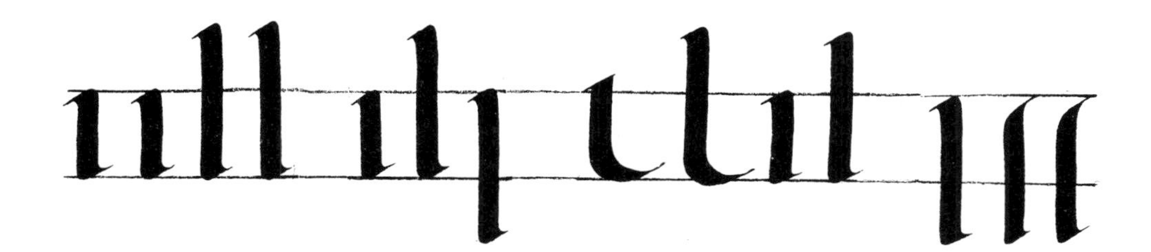

The letters of this alphabet are round and chunky, so the serifs should reflect this character. Holding your pen at a consistent 30° angle, begin at the top of the stroke with a small serif, pull straight down to the line and then lift off to the right.

Having mastered these marks you can now write several letters of the alphabet. Most letters are made up of a series of strokes so that the pen can be pulled rather than pushed. This not only gives you more control but also helps to build up the rhythm of the writing. Try Exercise 2, remembering to hold your pen at 30° and to pull strokes from left to right and from top to bottom.

Exercise 2

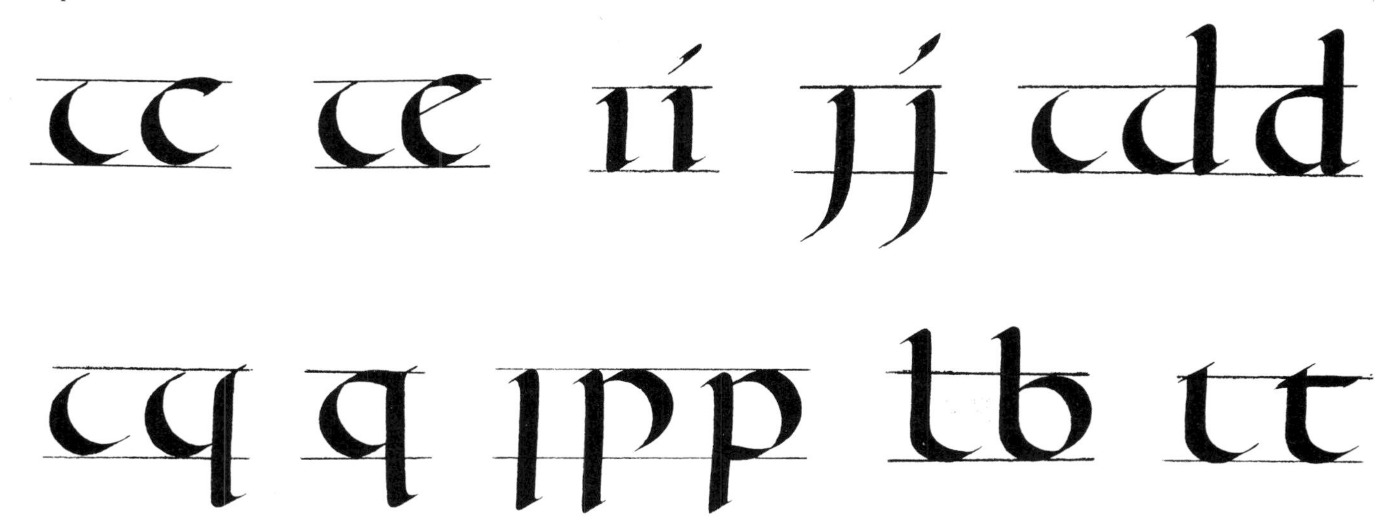

By repeating these three basic strokes but putting them together in different ways you have written 'o', 'c', 'e', 'd', 'q', 'l', 'p', 'b', 't', 'i' and 'j', and you can see how the pattern of the hand is beginning to emerge.

Because the basic shape underlying the letters of this hand is the circle, the shape of 'o' is particularly important. If you look at the 'o's you have written, you may be wondering where to look for the circle. The internal white space is oval, the circumference is a squashed circle, but each corner of your nib is writing a circle. It may help you to draw a better 'o' if you follow the left corner of your nib with your eye as you practise the letter.

Exercise 3 moves on to the next basic stroke of this hand, which is the arch. Most of the letters you have tried so far have part of the circle in them. The arched letters have only an arc of the circle.

Begin with an 'n'. Make a downstroke as you have already practised doing, put your pen back into that stroke just below the writing line, pull up and round just as if you were writing the second half of 'o', then pull down to the writing line.

Exercise 3

Now look at the white arch inside your letter. You are aiming to make it symmetrical and softly rounded, just like the Norman arches which were being built at the time the Ramsey Psalter was being written. This arch is repeated in a number of letters.

Now work carefully through Exercise 4.

Exercise 4

'm' is two arches, 'u' is an arch upside down and 'a' has an arch for its back. Write the arch of 'a', then put your pen into the stem about half way up, and in one stroke pull to the left and then curve round and back up into the stem.

As you can see, by adding one more basic stroke to your skills you have added six more letters to your alphabet.

Most of the letters which you have studied so far have fallen into two main groups: those which include half or more of the circle and those which use the arch shape. The third major group of letters uses a new mark, the diagonal stroke.

Work through Exercise 5, always remembering to pull the pen from the top line to the bottom. You will also notice that the pen is held at a different angle for these marks. Turn your hand so that the edge of your pen is at about 45° to the horizontal writing line.

Exercise 5

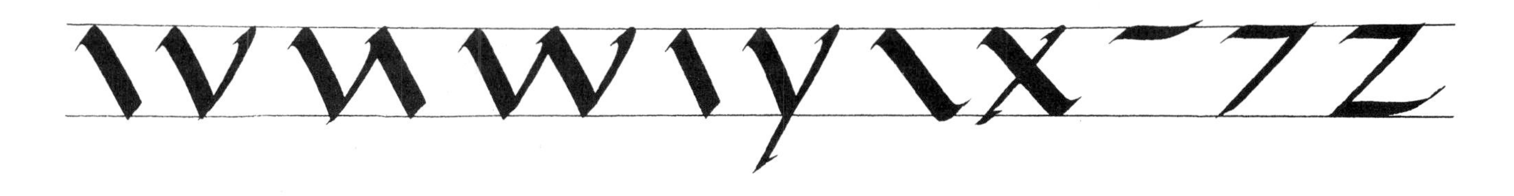

'w' is 'v' x 2 and 'y' is 'v' with a tail. At its widest point, 'v' should be about as wide as 'o' at its widest point. The reason for turning the pen will become clear if you try to write 'v' with your pen at 30°. Instead of a pleasing balance of one heavy and one lighter stroke, you will find that both strokes are heavy, the point of the 'v' is clumsy and blunt, and the letter looks rather coarse. If you look at the letters in Exercise 5 you will see that the pen angle is not consistent, but I have turned it as necessary to give a pleasing balance of thick and thin lines. It is essential to keep looking critically at what you are doing.

If you now look through the letters you have studied, you will realize that we have only a small group of oddments still to try. The patterns in Exercise 6 include some marks which you already know and a few variations. If you remember that a mark is always made from top to bottom and from left to right you will quickly master these last few letters.

Exercise 6

The top of 'f' is again an arc of the circle and 'k' is closely related to 'h'. 's' and 'g' are a little more idiosyncratic.

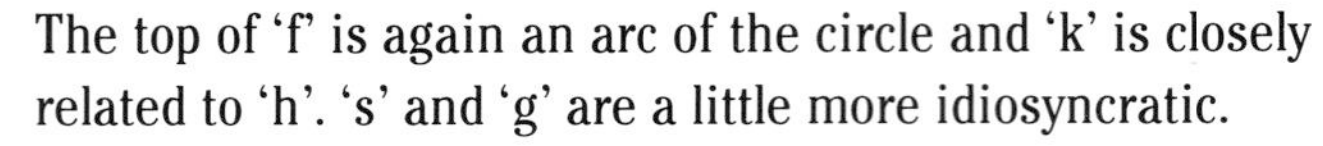

's' sits inside the 'o' circle; 'g' has a reduced circle for its top and a balancing wider oval for its base. It is interesting that this form of 'g', historically based but rarely found in modern written forms, is still regularly used in typefaces.

When analysed in this way, the alphabet ceases to be twenty-six complicated abstract shapes and becomes a series of simple marks rearranged to make up twenty-six letters. If you practise the letters in their pattern groups, always bearing in mind that you are repeating exactly the same mark in different letters, you will learn them quickly and your hand will remember the pattern shapes.

As soon as you have learned the shapes, go on to write words. Again you will learn faster if you use the patterns to help you, so begin by writing all the words you can think of with 'oo' in them, all the words which begin with 'ab', which end in 'y', which have 'bb', 'ss' or 'gg' in them. Practising letters will help you to learn shapes and the sequence of strokes, but writing words is the only effective way to learn the rhythm and pattern of the writing.

Letter and word spacing now becomes important. When writing a formal calligraphic hand, our usual aim is to communicate in a direct but aesthetic manner. We want our message to be clear and easily read and to look attractive without its appearance being a distraction. Our writing must be even and disciplined if it is to present this image.

When you move on to Exercise 7, begin by writing the word 'minimum' and try to make the white spaces, both inside the letters and between them, as equal as you can. Look at your writing upside down – is one of your white spaces larger than the others? Are your marks too close together? Try the other

words and the same test. You will probably find that letters need to be a little further apart than you expect.

When you have worked through the words in Exercise 7, write a sentence. Be careful not to leave too much space between your words, as this will interrupt the reading eye as it runs along the line.

Exercise 7

minimum

animal insect

pens and ink

writing

The Foundational hand is logical and ordered. It is made up of a few simple marks; most of the letters belong to three clearly defined groups, a few others adding a little variety without being too idiosyncratic. Any formal hand will take time to learn and true control of the pen may take a while to achieve, but if you understand the relationship between letters and the patterns of the writing, mastery will come the faster.

EXPERIMENTING WITH FOUNDATIONAL HAND

Formal calligraphic writing makes a pattern on the page. It is disciplined and controlled, it repeats elements but has enough variety to keep us interested. For these experiments to be useful, your writing should still have a pattern. Keep looking at your writing and thinking about how you are making it.

The writing of the Ramsey Psalter is strong, firm and vigorous – Edward Johnston called it 'brisk'; it is also clear and easy to read. A modern Foundational hand should have similar qualities.

It is important to take these characteristics into account when considering uses for this writing. Our first reaction to a piece of writing is visual – we see a pattern on a page – and we will have made any number of judgements about the text because of its presentation before we get close enough to read it. The size of writing, the colour, the weight of the marks, the shapes, the spaces, the margins, the confidence of the line are all elements to which we respond before we begin to read the words and take in their meaning.

So far we have studied marks and letter shapes and have written words. The next exercise must be to put words together, to write a piece of continuous text so that the texture and pattern made by this style of writing can be seen.

For the next few experiments, you will need a piece of text of about 15 words. It needn't be great literature, but it should be real sentences.

For Experiment 1, using a slightly smaller nib than you have used so far (I used a Rexel 1½), rule some writing guidelines which are four nib-widths apart, but this time leave a space between each pair of writing lines big enough to allow room for your ascenders and descenders. Try a space six nib-widths apart to begin with. Now write out your text as carefully as you can, dividing it into four short lines so that you have a block of writing. Try to space your letters evenly and don't leave big

Experiment 1

Season of mists
and mellow fruitfulness

gaps between the words. This will give you a clearer picture of what a piece of writing in Foundational hand looks like. As you can see, it is plain and straightforward, clear and unfussy, round, solid and friendly.

So far in all your studies of this hand you have followed the same basic principles about the pen angle, the weight of letter and the letter form, and you have learned one style of writing. Edward Johnston suggested that Foundational hand 'forms an excellent general basis for further development'. In fact, any classic calligraphic hand can be adapted with just a little experimentation. If you continue to use the same nib for the following exercises, you will begin to see that an endless variety of styles of formal writing can be based on just one classic hand.

For Experiment 2, rule some guidelines five nib-widths apart and with an eight nib-widths gap between each pair. Keeping your pen at 30° and the letters round and even, write out your piece of text again. As you can see, the letters are larger, lighter and more airy, taking up much more space. The character of the writing has changed.

Experiment 2

mellow
fruitfulness

Now repeat the exercise for Experiment 3, but this time with writing lines three nib-widths apart and with a six nib-widths gap between the lines. Again the character of the writing has changed – it has become dense and heavy.

Experiment 3

mellow fruitfulness

Look back at the photograph of the Ramsey Psalter on page 27 and you will see that the writing slopes. This is a quality of fluent, confident writing, but don't let the slope become too marked because this will make your writing illegible.

If you compare the three pieces of writing which you have done so far, you will see that just by altering one of the basic principles very slightly, you have created three quite different 'looks' on the page.

It is perfectly possible to experiment further with the weight of the letters and to try writing at two nib-widths high or at six, eight or ten nib-widths high. Some interesting ideas would come of this, although very light or very heavy writing is usually harder to read. If our aim is clear, legible writing, the Foundational hand is probably most successful at about four nib-widths high, but remember that legibility is not always the prime concern; writing is a tool to be used and adapted to suit different purposes.

Experiment 4 is written between lines four nib-widths apart, but this time the angle of the pen has been changed to between 10° and 15°. The writing looks heavier and more static; it has lost some of its vigour.

Experiment 4

mellow
fruitfulness

Something similar has happened in Experiment 5. Rule lines four nib-widths apart and write with the pen at 30°, but instead of finishing the strokes with a curved serif, lift your pen and add a separate stroke for the serif. This is a very small change to the basic hand, but the serifs make it look a little more formal.

Experiment 5

mellow
fruitfulness

Pages 40-41. *These experiments are all based on Foundational hand. The very different looks of the writing have been created by holding the pen at different angles, by compressing the letters so that the shapes become oval rather than round, and by changing the weights of the letters.*

For Experiment 6 the pen is held at 30° and the letters are four nib-widths high, but the basic shape has been altered. Instead of a round 'o' and circular letter shapes, the letters have been stretched sideways. This opens up the texture of the writing and makes it look lighter, but it also, I think, makes the writing look slower, which is why I chose a different piece of text.

Experiment 6

mellow
fruitfulness

Instead of being stretched, the basic letter shape in Experiment 7 is squashed from circular to oval, which again makes a different 'look' on the page. This writing has lost its soft, round shapes and although it looks quite strong it also looks a bit stiff and rigid.

Experiment 7

mellow fruitfulness

You can see from these experiments that by altering just one of the three basic principles of a formal hand, you can make the style look very different; in effect you are inventing a new hand each time. By understanding one hand you have given yourself enough knowledge and skill to develop as many new ways of writing as you wish. What matters is that you should understand what you are doing and be creating writing which is aesthetic and appropriate.

autumn

autu

autumn

seasons

autur

autumn

autumn

aul autumn

AUTUMN

original

a · autun

autum · a

summer ·

summer

GETTING TO KNOW PAPER

Calligraphy is writing and writing is words, sentences, communication. It is obviously important at the beginning to learn to write your letters as well as you can, but learning these letters is a means to an end, not an end in itself. As soon as possible, use your writing to make something real. It may be as simple as labels for homemade wine or marmalade, a notice for the school or a small greetings card, but whatever you choose, you will have to move on from your layout pad, probably to more serious, better paper.

Paper comes in three varieties – machine-made, mould-made and handmade. Handmade paper is hard to find and often, because it has its own personality, difficult to write on; mould-made papers are sold in good art shops and many are useful for calligraphy. Most paper is made by machine but it rarely has the archival qualities which artists and calligraphers need.

The range of papers available can seem bewildering and the best ways to learn are to browse around art shops, look in catalogues and compare notes with friends. If you paint, sketch or draw, you will be familiar with many of the papers which calligraphers use. I usually work on watercolour paper which is mould-made, of archival quality and has a smooth, hot-pressed surface, but all calligraphers have their own favourites and you will be no exception.

You should choose your paper according to its colour and its surface. You will write more easily on paper which is smooth but not too shiny – if it is too glossy the ink will slide about on it. Rough paper can create some interesting textures, but is no use for simple formal writing. It is always wise to buy large sheets of paper. This is usually more economical and you can trim margins down, but you can't stick bits on.

The thickness of paper is described in terms of its weight in grammes per square metre. Choose the weight of your paper carefully; too heavy a paper might look coarse and may be hard to write on, whereas thin paper will crack and crease very easily, producing a messy piece of work.

Opposite page. *A selection of papers. The plain sheets include a piece of blue-grey handmade English paper, a white mould-made watercolour paper which has a rough surface and some sheets of handmade Indian papers. The rolls include handmade Japanese papers, marbled papers including some hand-marbled by Renate Eising, and two sheets of machine-made decorative Japanese papers.*

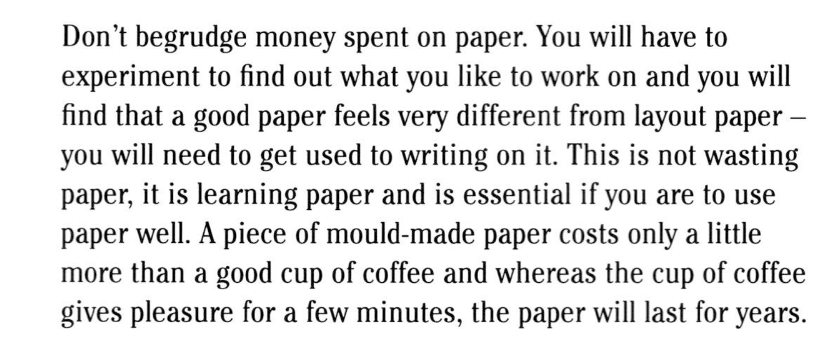

Don't begrudge money spent on paper. You will have to experiment to find out what you like to work on and you will find that a good paper feels very different from layout paper – you will need to get used to writing on it. This is not wasting paper, it is learning paper and is essential if you are to use paper well. A piece of mould-made paper costs only a little more than a good cup of coffee and whereas the cup of coffee gives pleasure for a few minutes, the paper will last for years.

Because paper is made from fibres and the fibres tend to settle in one direction, a sheet of paper has a grain. Take a sheet of writing paper and lay it on a table. Lift one short end, take it over and lay it on the other short end so that both ends are laid flat together on the table and the rest of the sheet is curved. With your other hand feel the strength of the bounce in the curve. Now repeat the exercise, this time laying long edge against long edge and feeling the bounce. One bounce will feel much stronger than the other and if you fold the paper so that you crease the weaker bounce, the paper will crease easily and will lie flat. Always test your paper this way and crease with the softer bounce – that is, with the grain.

This is particularly important when making cards or books.

PROJECT – TO MAKE A SMALL BOOK

The idea for a little book of weather rhymes was prompted by a calligraphy exhibition on the theme of the natural world. Writing based on Foundational hand seemed appropriate for the rhymes, which are traditional, short and direct. Having collected about twenty rhymes from which to choose, I made a sheet of quick lettering experiments.

Having worked through this sheet of experiments, which was done on a handmade Indian paper, I made further colour trials on different papers and as a result I made my decisions about letter forms, colour scheme, scale of writing and paper.

The next stage was to plan the pages of the book. This was done as a very rough mock-up on layout paper.

Next I tested the grain of my sheet of Indian paper and then carefully measured the pages, marking the edges lightly in pencil. I then wrote the book before I folded it. I had to make one join as my paper wasn't long enough and the wrap-around cover was also added as an extra piece of paper.

The sheet of Indian paper had an inconsistent surface and the writing is consequently a bit bumpy, but I decided that this was in keeping with the character of the paper and the book, which is informal, easy to handle and easy to make.

The paper is an essential ingredient in any piece of work and it must be chosen with thought and care. Experiment with as many different papers as you can, remembering that different contexts demand different materials. Paper is a very seductive material and it is worth learning to use it well.

A selection of the first lettering experiments done on Indian handmade paper and using a variety of colours.

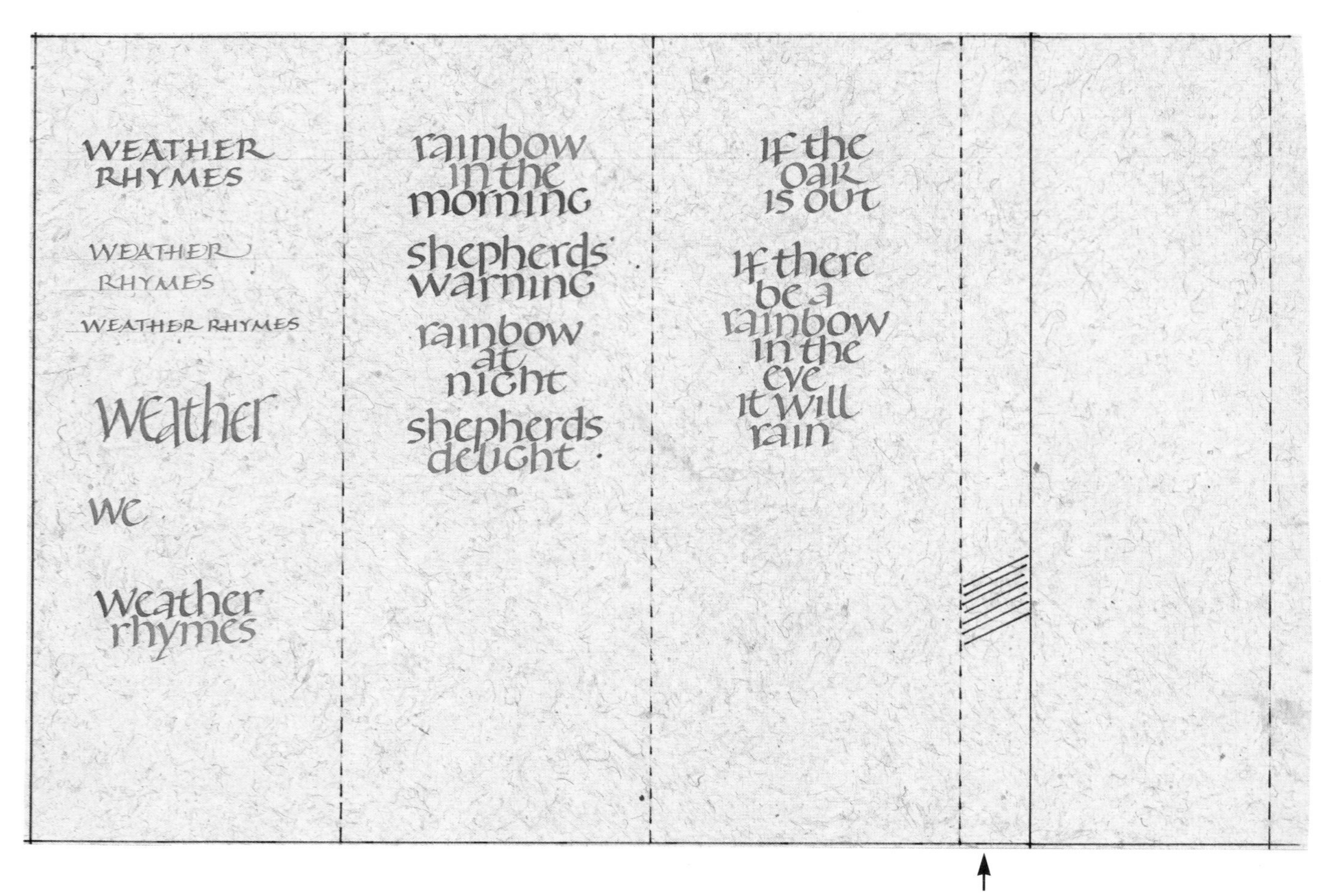

Above. *A draft for the concertina book of weather rhymes using gouache on handmade Indian paper. I tried several different ideas for the title page before deciding to use the same style of writing as for the rest of the book.*

To join two pages, add a small hem about 20mm (¾ in deep) to one page. This hem is then glued to the underside of the next page. The dotted lines mark the folds; the shaded area becomes the hem.

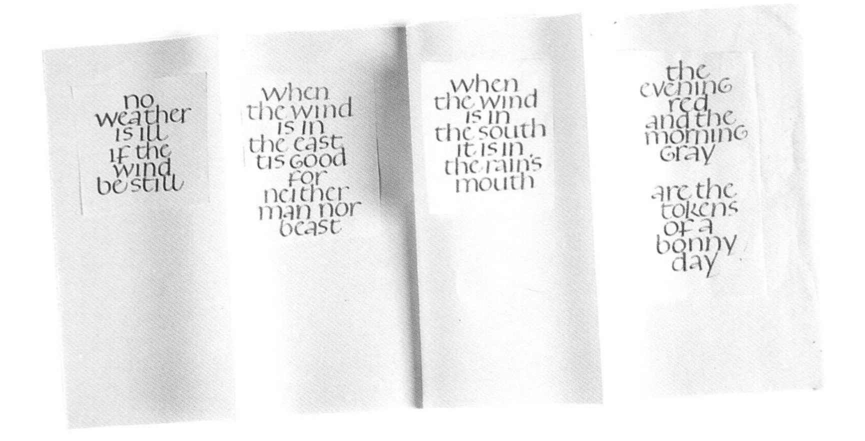

Right. *The first rough paste-up for the book. I cut layout paper to the same size as the book and folded it into a concertina shape. I then wrote the blocks of text on layout paper, cut them out and placed them carefully on to my mock-up of the book to get the position right. This layout was then copied for the real book.*

The completed book. Gouache on Indian handmade paper, finished with a ribbon tie. The text blocks fold together and the cover then wraps round the complete book. Page size 230 x 80mm (9 x 3¼ in).

PEN-MADE CAPITALS – STEP-BY-STEP

Most calligraphers will tell you that the model for classic Roman capital letters is the inscription on Trajan's Column. This structure, dating from about AD 113 and standing in Trajan's Forum in Rome, carries a carved inscription commemorating the victories of the Emperor Trajan.

The letters are indeed extremely handsome Roman capitals. They are also incised and generally about 110mm (4½ in) high. Many scholars think that they were first drawn out with a brush and then carved with a chisel. So what have these letters to do with pen-made calligraphic letters?

The calligrapher usually works at a relatively small scale. The written mark is made directly on to the page – put pen to paper and the mark is there and cannot be changed – and the variety of thick and thin strokes is created by the broad-edged writing instrument. The pen can only produce a rather distant approximation of an incised Roman capital letter. What calligraphers can do is to take the proportions and basic shapes of these Roman capitals and adapt them for use with calligraphic tools and materials.

Moulding from Trajan's Column now in the Victoria and Albert Museum, London. The letters are approximately 110mm (4½ in) high.

The letters on Trajan's Column are handsome and well made, but much of their quality comes from the visual harmony between the letters. Look at each letter individually and it appears strong and well balanced within itself, but it also sits comfortably with its neighbours, creating a firm, regular texture. There are enough similarities between shapes and proportions of letters to give a sense of a pleasing pattern, but there is also enough variety to stimulate interest.

These letters have been studied and analysed by both artists and academics. To use them as the starting point for pen-made letters, the calligrapher must also analyse and rationalize. It is important to appreciate that the diagrams which follow are a rationalization.

The diagrams show the relative proportions of the letters in monoline. All the letters of the alphabet have been related to a circle, which is one of the reasons why these capitals are used with Foundational hand.

The diameter of the circle equals one side of the square. The rectangle has the same area as the circle. The short side of the rectangle is approximately three-quarters of the diameter of the circle. The total shaded red area is equal to the shaded blue area.

Capital letters analysed by this method fall into four groups according to their widths. The round letters are 'O', 'C', 'G', 'Q', 'D'.

'O' is a perfect circle.

'Q' is a perfect circle with a tail. When written with a broad nib the tail of 'Q' begins where the letter is at its thinnest.

'C' is almost a full circle, but it stops when it meets the side of the rectangle. The top and bottom curves are a little flattened as they finish.

'G' is made like 'C', but with the addition of a flat half side.

'D' has the side of the rectangle for its back and uses the right side of the circle.

The following diagrams show the underlying geometric construction of pen-made Roman capital letters and their relative proportions. The diameter of the circle is the same length as the side of the square. The shorter side of the rectangle is three-quarters of the diameter of the circle. The diagrams were made with compasses and a ruler.

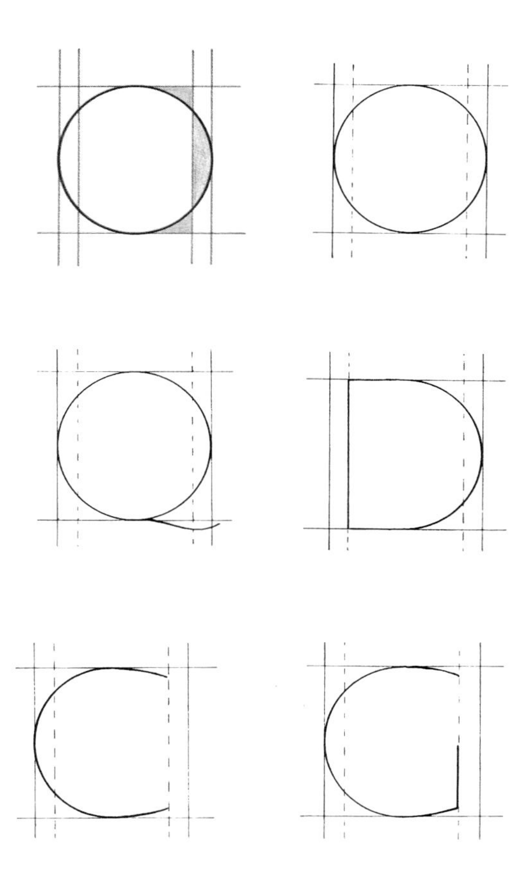

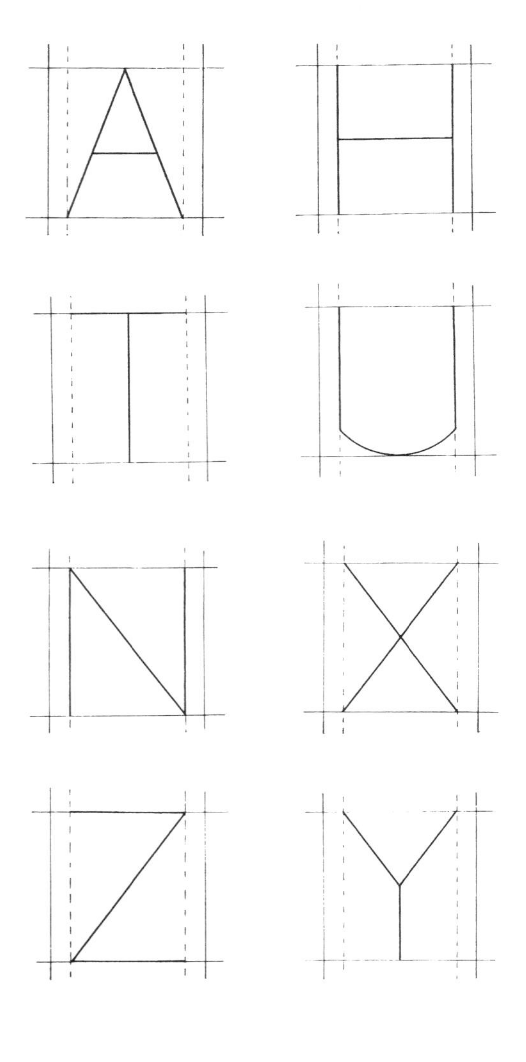

The rectangular letters are ‘A’, ‘H’, ‘T’, ‘U’, ‘N’, ‘X’, ‘Z’, ‘Y’, ‘V’.

The area of the rectangle is the same as that of the circle, so these letters are using the same space as the circular letters.

‘A’ ‘H’ The difference between the cross bars of ‘A’ and ‘H’ is necessary because of the internal proportions of the letters.

‘V’ ‘Z’ ‘X’ ‘X’ crosses in the centre of the rectangle, ‘V’ pierces the bottom line at the centre point.

‘U’ is the only letter in this group which uses the rectangle and the circle.

‘N’ uses the sides of the rectangle.

‘Y’ ‘T’ The stem of ‘T’ is in the centre of the rectangle and the junction of ‘Y’ is at the centre point.

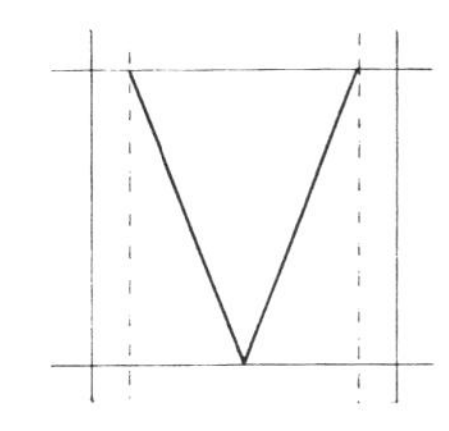

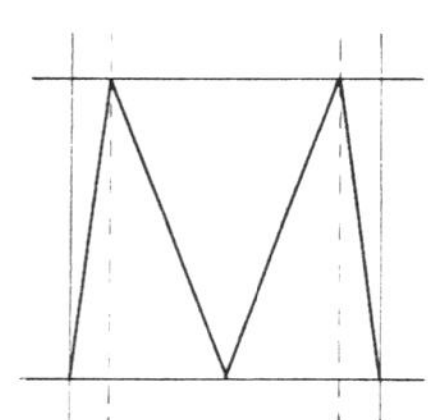

The wide letters are ‘M’ and ‘W’.

‘M’ uses the full width of the square. The centre is a ‘V’ and the outer legs complete the square.

‘W’ is formed by placing two ‘V’s side by side.

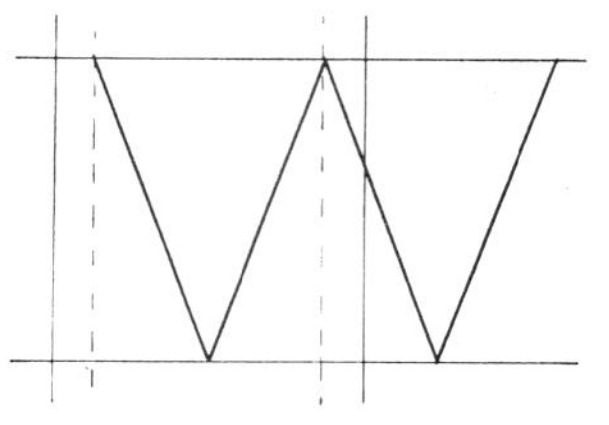

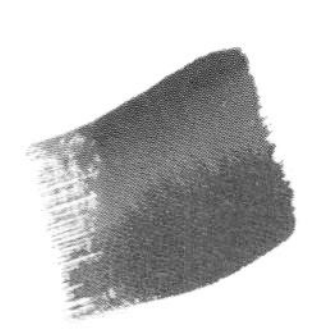

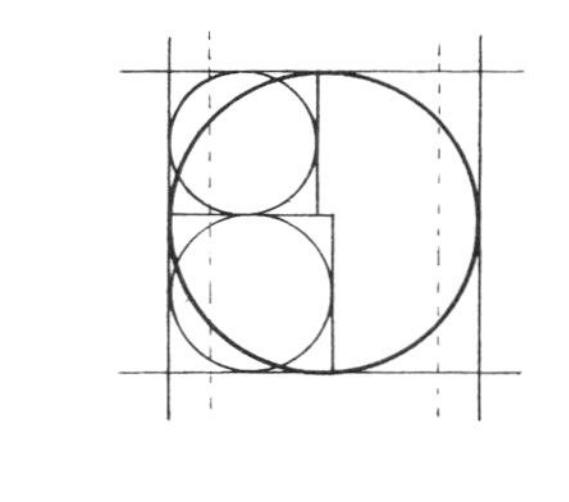

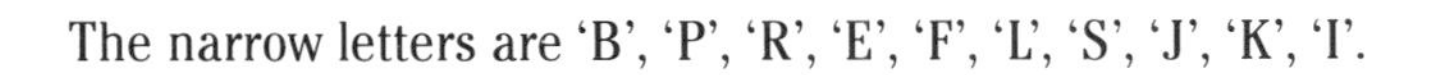

The narrow letters are 'B', 'P', 'R', 'E', 'F', 'L', 'S', 'J', 'K', 'I'.

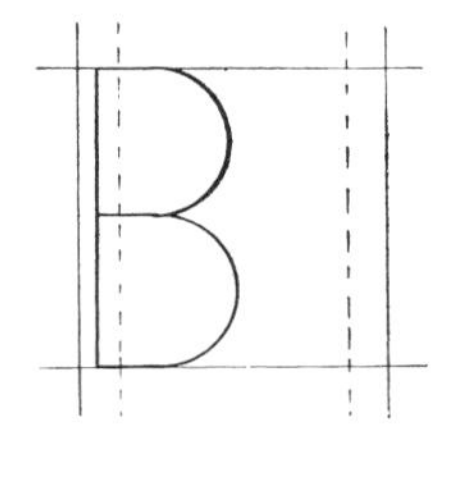

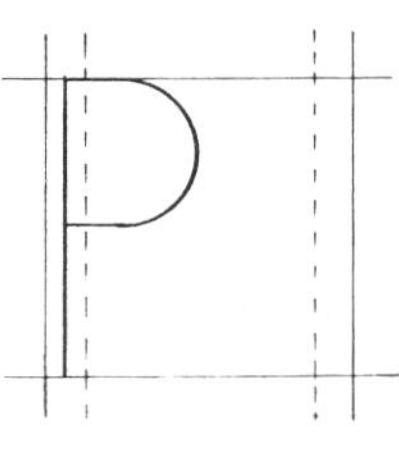

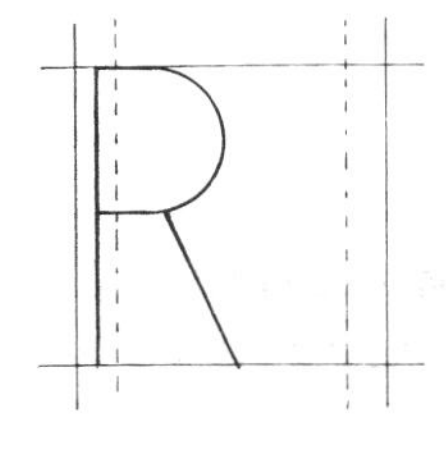

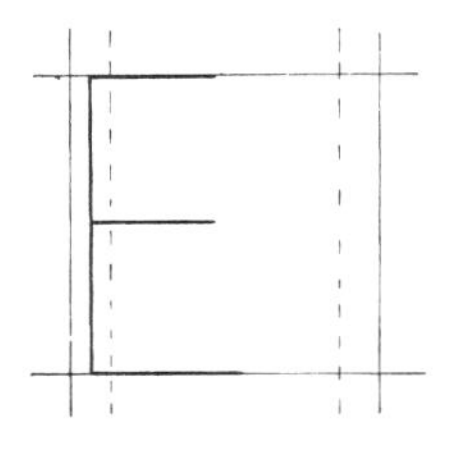

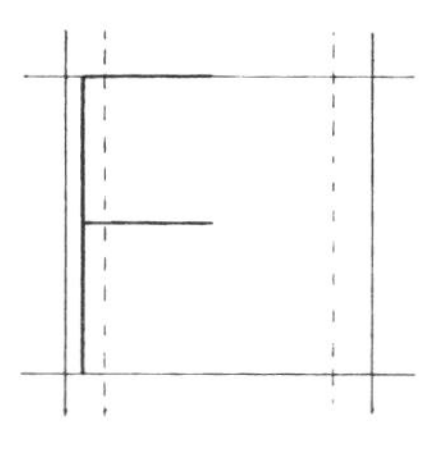

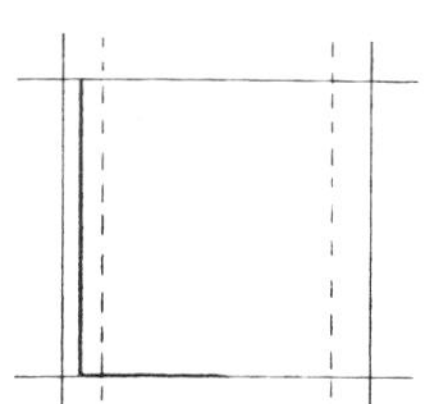

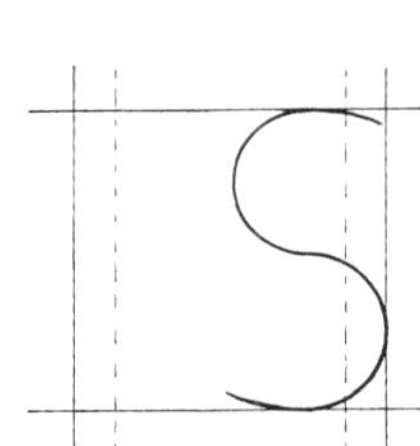

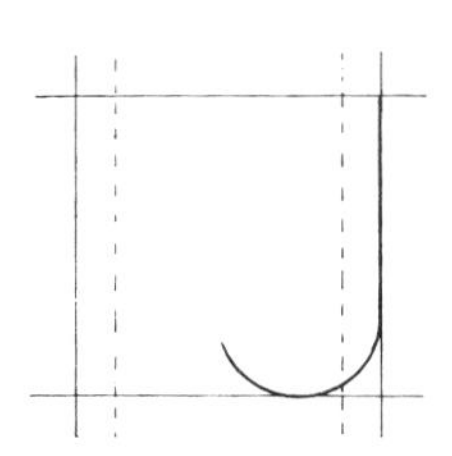

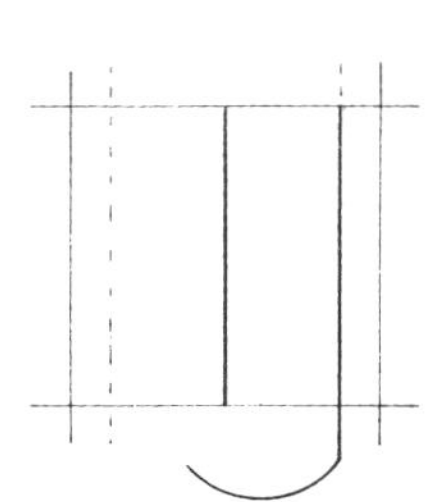

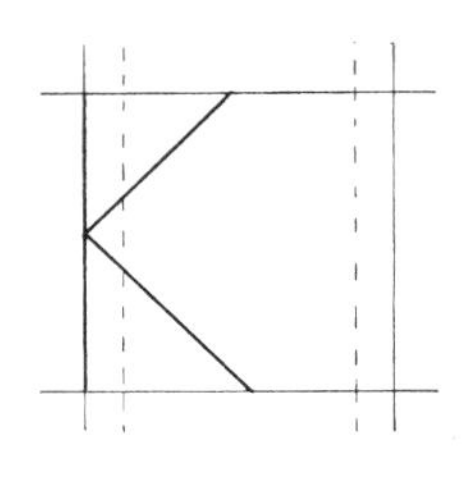

Most of the narrow letters have a waist just above the centre point, so two smaller circles and squares have been added to the original diagram.

'B' 'P' 'R' The difference in size between the top and bottom circles is minimal but significant.

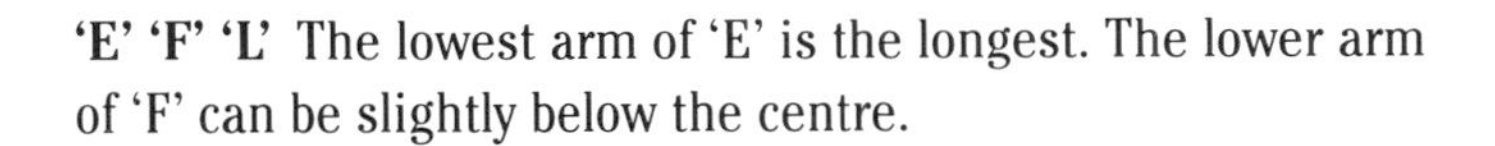

'E' 'F' 'L' The lowest arm of 'E' is the longest. The lower arm of 'F' can be slightly below the centre.

'S' 'J' 'S' follows the edges of the two circles. 'J' can be more substantial and drop below the bottom line.

'I' is a single stroke. Notice that historically it has no top or bottom horizontal strokes.

'K' The two arms of 'K' form a right angle just about the centre point.

These geometric structures underlie the pen-made letters which are the next study.

For the first exercise you will need a large nib once more and some pencil guidelines ruled seven nib-widths apart. Just as with the lower case letters, capital letters use repeated marks and are constructed from a series of strokes, always pulled from top to bottom and from left to right.

Holding the pen at an angle of 30°, write a capital 'O' between your guidelines. It is made exactly like a Foundational 'o' but is larger. Now use that same first stroke of the circle to write 'Q', 'C' and 'G'.

'D' is a little different because it uses the second stroke of the circle.

Remember to stop when your pen begins to push, and to pull your final stroke from left to right. Practise these letters until you are at ease with them.

Exercise 1

The second exercise moves on to the rectangular group of letters. First try 'H', 'U' and 'T', keeping the serifs small and rounded as you did for Foundational hand.

Exercise 2

For the rest of the rectangular letters you will need to hold your pen at steeper angles to keep a pleasing balance between the thick and thin diagonal strokes. Write 'A', 'V', 'X', 'N', 'Y' and 'Z'.

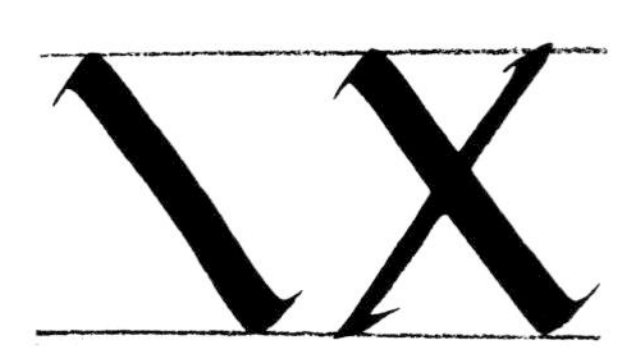

If you look carefully at these letters you will see that my pen angle is not consistent, but alters as necessary to create a balance between thick and thin strokes.

Remember that these letters are as wide as each other at their widest point and 'H' is three-quarters the width of 'O'.

Now try Exercise 3 and the wide letters, again using a steeper pen angle.

Exercise 3

Keep the legs of 'M' fairly straight and don't be afraid of 'W': it is a very wide letter.

When you are ready, move on to Exercise 4 and the narrow group of letters. If you remember to pull the pen from left to right, the sequence of strokes will be clear. Write 'P', 'R', 'B', 'K', 'L', 'E', 'F', 'I', 'J' and 'S'.

Exercise 4

Right. *From* The Sunne Rising *by John Donne. Gouache and watercolour on hot pressed watercolour paper. The gold leaf was laid on gum ammoniac and the decoration added with a stencilling brush. Reproduced real size.*

Having worked through all the letters of the alphabet, practise writing them in their related groups until you are thoroughly familiar with the shapes and proportions. It is useful to return regularly to write an 'O' so that you can check that the proportions of your letters still relate to the circle; you should also keep checking that the letters within each group relate to each other.

Choose a short sentence and write it carefully in capitals. Try to space your letters and words evenly as you did when writing lower case Foundational hand.

Finally, look back at the photograph of Trajan's Column and compare those letters with the ones you have been studying. You will now be able to see some significant differences.

As I said at the beginning of this study, large letters carved in stone have to be adapted if they are to be written with a small pen on paper. Rationalizing the letters into four related groups helps to create a more regular pattern which is close to the natural movements and rhythms of writing. These pen-made capitals retain some of the characteristics of the Trajan's Column letters while being entirely appropriate to pen, ink and paper.

BUSIE
OLD FOOLE
UNRULY
SUNNE

WHY DOST
THOU THUS
THROUGH
WINDOWES
AND THROUGH
CURTAINES
CALL
ON US

CAPITALS IN CONTEXT

We expect to see written or printed capital letters used singly, such as to mark the beginning of a sentence or to denote a proper name. However, we are not surprised to meet complete words or texts in capitals in certain contexts. Headlines in newspapers, the titles of books, films and magazines, the names of shops and of products, the texts on plaques, foundation stones and memorials are frequently printed, painted or carved in capital letters.

This suggests that our response to the formal Roman capital letter hasn't changed much since Trajan's Column was carved around AD 113. We see capitals as important letters and we use them when we want to impress or to emphasize that what we are saying matters.

Having learned the letter shapes for a classic capital letter, we must now assess the visual impact of these letters when they are used for complete words and sentences.

First roughs for a piece to be written in Roman capitals trying out different colours, line and letter spacings.

For the first experiment you will be using your large nib and guidelines which are seven nib-widths apart. Choose a

ID ID ARBITROR AD PRIME

ID ARBITROR ESSE UTILE
ADRIME
IN VITA
ESSE UT NEQUID NEMIS

ARBITROR ADPRIME

UT NEQUID NEMIS

ID·ARBITROR
ADPRIME
IN·VITA
ESSE·UTILE
UT·NEQUID
NEMIS

sentence of about ten or twelve words which suits the character of Roman capitals and write it out between the guidelines. Then write it again with the words stacked below one another. Leave a small space of about two nib-widths between your lines of writing.

The pen-written letter cannot equal the visual strength of a letter carved in stone, but as you can now see, a piece of writing in pen-made capital letters does look more important than a passage written in minuscules. It has a certain dignity and formality.

This experiment also shows why the relative proportions of capitals are so important. These letters are of a uniform height and have no ascenders and descenders as minuscule letters do. The pattern formed by the letters comes from the variations in their widths and shapes. As you saw in the

A finished piece of work in pen-made Roman capitals which grew out of Experiment 1. The line spacing has been kept quite close but as capital letters are of a uniform height the lines of text are perfectly legible.

/ CAPITALS

/CAPITALS

/CAPITALS

/ CAPITALS

/ CAPITALS

/ CAPITALS

/ CAPITALS

/ CAPITALS

Experiment 2

earlier studies, there are important similarities between certain letters, which create the writing pattern, and important differences, which create the variety.

This basic form of capital letter is immensely useful and sits very well with the Foundational letters already studied. It is also a very versatile letter form and can be adapted almost endlessly to create different visual images for use in a wide range of contexts.

For Experiment 2 you will be trying out some different weights of capital letters. Still using a fairly large nib (all my examples were written with a No. 1 Rexel nib), rule some guidelines eight nib-widths apart and write a few words between them in capitals. Now repeat this with guidelines nine nib-widths apart. Try to maintain the letter shapes and proportions which you have learned. You may be surprised to see how much larger your writing becomes. At nine nib-widths high, it appears much more airy and spacious and it takes up considerably more room.

Now, using the same nib and the same words, increase the weight of the letters step by step. Rule guidelines six nib-widths apart, then five and so on down to two nib-widths apart. The appearance of your letters will change significantly and quickly and you can see that as the letters get smaller and heavier it is only possible to maintain legibility by allowing them to become wider.

Now look carefully at the different styles of capital letter which you have created simply by changing the letter height. The conventional weight of letter with which you began is easy to read and looks formal and dignified. The other styles which you have created have different characters and will be useful in a wide variety of calligraphic contexts.

So far all your writing has been controlled by guidelines. Pencil guidelines are scaffolding, a support system. They are essential in the early stages of a study when your hand is learning the size of the letter and your eye is learning its weight and proportions, but when these skills are developed, the scaffolding becomes unnecessary and may even be a handicap to you.

For Experiment 3 take the same nib and a blank sheet of layout paper and write out the words which you have been using in Experiment 2 directly and freely, without pencil guidelines. Try to maintain the shapes and weight of the basic formal capitals with which you began and keep your spacing as even as possible.

You may be surprised to find how straight your lines of working are, but you will also see whether you tend to stretch or shrink your letters, which ones you are really confident about and which you have not yet fully learned and need to practise more.

The next step is to allow the letters to relax a little. I suggest that for Experiment 4 you return to your seven nib-widths high guidelines, choose a letter which you enjoy writing and experiment with it. Try stretching and squeezing your letter, changing your pen angle, allowing the strokes to break through the guidelines and using different serifs.

Don't worry about making beautiful marks – try anything which comes into your mind. One of the best ways to find ideas is to allow yourself to doodle, but to doodle thoughtfully. Look at what you are producing. Much of it you will reject because you find it ugly, but there will certainly be some good ideas on your pages and you will find a use for them when the time is right.

When you have enough confidence, the next step is to allow yourself to experiment with a single letter, using as many different tools, materials and colours as possible.

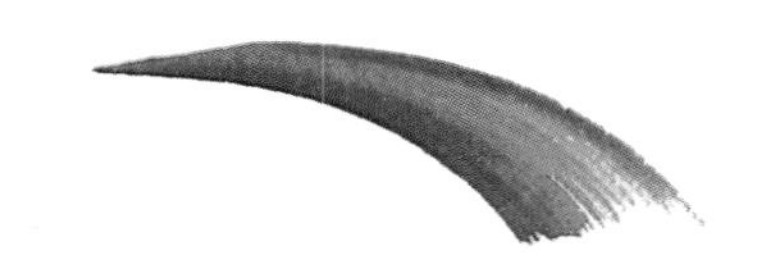

Roughs for 'Zed'. The first ideas were written very quickly using a variety of tools and were gradually refined as the idea for the finished piece began to take shape.

This is how I began work on 'Zed'. As you can see from the examples, the first ideas were little more than scribbles. I used a variety of large pens, small nibs, wedge-shaped brushes, felt-tips and pencils, always trying to make marks rhythmically and with the essential characteristics of 'Z' still showing through.

Opposite page. *Three finished versions of 'Zed' all written in gouache on watercolour paper.*

I worked on a number of different paper surfaces, tried a variety of colours and wasn't worried about making a mess. I find this a very useful way to get ideas flowing, because I constantly evaluate what I am doing. I liked the strong colour texture made by the large pen, but decided to use the softer mark of the wedge-shaped brush for the finished piece. The initial ideas were then refined down to one tool, one surface and one shape of letter.

I wrote several sheets of 'Z's until I had five letters to use in the finished piece of work. I added the red flourish with a small pen to create a contrast between the large, soft line of the brush and the small, firm pen mark.

Right. *Brush and steel nib, 630 x 190mm (25 x 7½ in) including the mount.* Below. *The first piece, written with a steel pen, looks more dramatic and harsh than the softer brush-made example below it. Text areas 110 x 180mm and 110 x 190mm (4½ x 7¼ in and 4½ x 7½ in) respectively.*

THOU·WHORESON·ZED
THOU·UNNECESSARY·LETTER
KING·LEAR

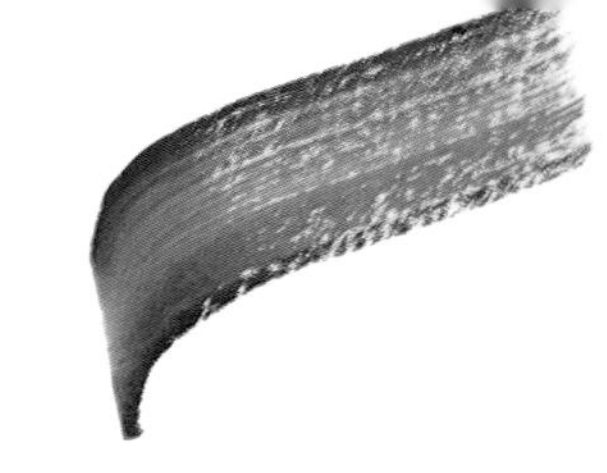

PROJECT – A GOOD LUCK CARD

One of the simplest but most effective ways to make a greetings card for a friend is to use the initial of his or her name. Begin by experimenting freely with the letter to get your ideas to flow. When you have made a variety of marks and images, you can then select and develop those ideas which are appropriate for your purpose. Different letter forms convey different visual messages and the reason for sending your card will help to make the decision for you. What event is the card marking? Is it a happy occasion or does it call for something more serious?

Bold colours and simple marks might be appropriate for a child's birthday card, but a thank you to a favourite aunt could suggest something small and exquisite. If the recipient is a friend with a passion for purple, perhaps this could be reflected in your colour scheme. A card of congratulations or in celebration of a landmark birthday might suggest something large and lively, but if your card has to be posted, keep its dimensions reasonable.

The card illustrated was made to wish a friend good luck. Using some of the ideas which grew out of the last experiments with 'Z', I worked on the letter 'J', using various combinations of blues and keeping the letter small and neat. I wrote the letters with a wedge-shaped brush, which makes a softer mark than a large steel nib. The shape of the letter had to be refined and many trials were rejected.

From the results I chose a few letters and then experimented with some free flourishes to add vigour to the design.

To make the card, I folded a piece of the same paper on which I had been doing my writing and cut four small diagonal slits in the front so that I could slot the finished J into them. The message was then written inside in tiny capital letters.

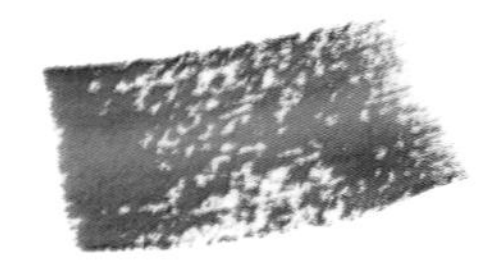

The letter 'J' was written in gouache with a 12.5mm (½in) wedge-shaped brush on NOT watercolour paper. The brush is held just like a broad-edged pen, but it needs a very different touch because it is so soft. The flourish was then added using a small steel nib. Reproduced real size.

ITALIC WRITING – A STUDY

Italic writing has its roots in the Renaissance and, as its name suggests, in what is now called Italy. It came into its own shortly after the invention of printing and I suspect that this timing is responsible for some of the characteristics of this particular hand.

Italic is essentially a rhythmic, flowing hand which can be written at some speed, important if you were a scribe competing with the new printing technology or coping with the increasing flow of paperwork from the Pope's office and other administrations. Its clean, simple shapes were adopted by some of the early writing masters and some of the earliest designers of typefaces.

If you look up examples of italic writing in a book of Renaissance manuscripts, you will see that its 'rules' were inconsistent. The letter forms varied, as did the weight of the letters and the way in which the pen was held. These variations, as you have seen in the experiments with Foundational hand and with capitals, significantly affect the character of the writing.

With any study of a formal calligraphic hand, it is important to use a real piece of writing as your starting point. There is a book of Bembo's Italian sonnets in the Victoria and Albert Museum in London. Pietro Bembo (1470-1547) was an Italian humanist, a cardinal and a writer of prose and poetry in both Latin and Italian. This book of his sonnets was written out for

S e de le mie ricchezze care et tante
Et si guardate; ond'io buon tempo uiſsi
Di mia sorte contento, et meco diſsi
Neſsun uiue di me piu lieto amante;
I o ſteſso mi disarmo: et queſte piante
A uezze a gir pur la; dou'io scopriſsi
Quegli occhi uaghi, et l'harmonia sentiſsi
De le parole si soaui et sante;
L ungi da lei di mio uoler sen'uanno:
Laſso chi mi dara Bernardo aita?
O chi m'acquetera, quand'io m'affanno?
M orrommi: et tu dirai mia fine udita;
Queſti, per non ueder il suo gran danno,
Laſciata la sua donna uscio di uita.

S ignor, che parti et tempri gli elementi,
E'l sole et l'altre ſtelle e'l mondo reggi,
Et hor col freno tuo santo correggi
Il lungo error de le mie uoglie ardenti;
N on lasciar la mia guardia, et non s'allenti
La tua pieta; perch'io tolto a le leggi
M'habbia d'amor, et diſturbato i seggi,
In ch'ei di me regnaua alti et lucenti.
C he come audace lupo suol de gli agni
Stretti nel chiuso lor; cosi coſtui
R itenta far di me l'usata preda.
A ccio pur dunque in danno i miei guadagni
Non torni, e'l lume tuo ſpegner si creda;
Con fermo pie dipartimi da lui.

C he come audace lupo suol de gli agni
Stretti nel chiuso lor; cosi coſtui
R itenta far di me l'usata preda.
A ccio pur dunque in danno i miei guadagni
Non torni, e'l lume tuo ſpegner si creda;
Con fermo pie dipartimi da lui.

Lisabetta Quirini in about 1543 by an unknown scribe. The page is small – approximately 215mm x 140mm or 8½in x 6½in – and the writing is tiny and immaculate. This book is an excellent starting point for the study of the italic hand, not only because it is clear and simple with few idiosyncratic shapes or marks, but because it is elegant and beautifully written. We are studying real writing of great skill and craftsmanship.

Opposite page. *A page from Bembo's Italian sonnets. London, Victoria and Albert Museum, Ms. L1347–1957. Written in Italy around 1543. Page size 215 x 140mm (8½ x 5½ in). Reproduced real size and with six lines enlarged.*

To begin your study of italic writing, prepare pencil guidelines which are five nib-widths apart, using a medium-sized nib. All writing has a natural scale and as you can see from the reproduction of the Bembo sonnets, early italic writing was often very small. However, to make a detailed study you must work large, so that you can really see what you are doing. I used a No. 1½ Rexel nib for these diagrams.

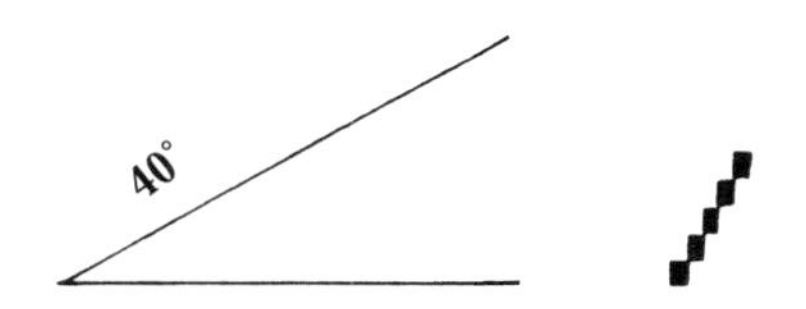

For this version of italic the weight of the letters is five nib-widths high, the pen is held at an angle of about 40° and the basic letter shape is oval. The other essential quality of italic is the rhythm which allows the writer's hand to move along relatively quickly.

Exercise 1

Hold your pen at about 40° to the writing line and reproduce the patterns shown in the first exercise. Try to make the shapes as regular and uniform as possible. If you feel the shapes with your hand as you write them, you will soon realize why the letters have this weight and form. It is easier to write more quickly with the pen held at a steeper angle because the friction on the surface of the paper is reduced. You will probably feel that your hand skims more easily over the surface of the paper. This naturally leads the hand and the eye to make taller but more compressed letters.

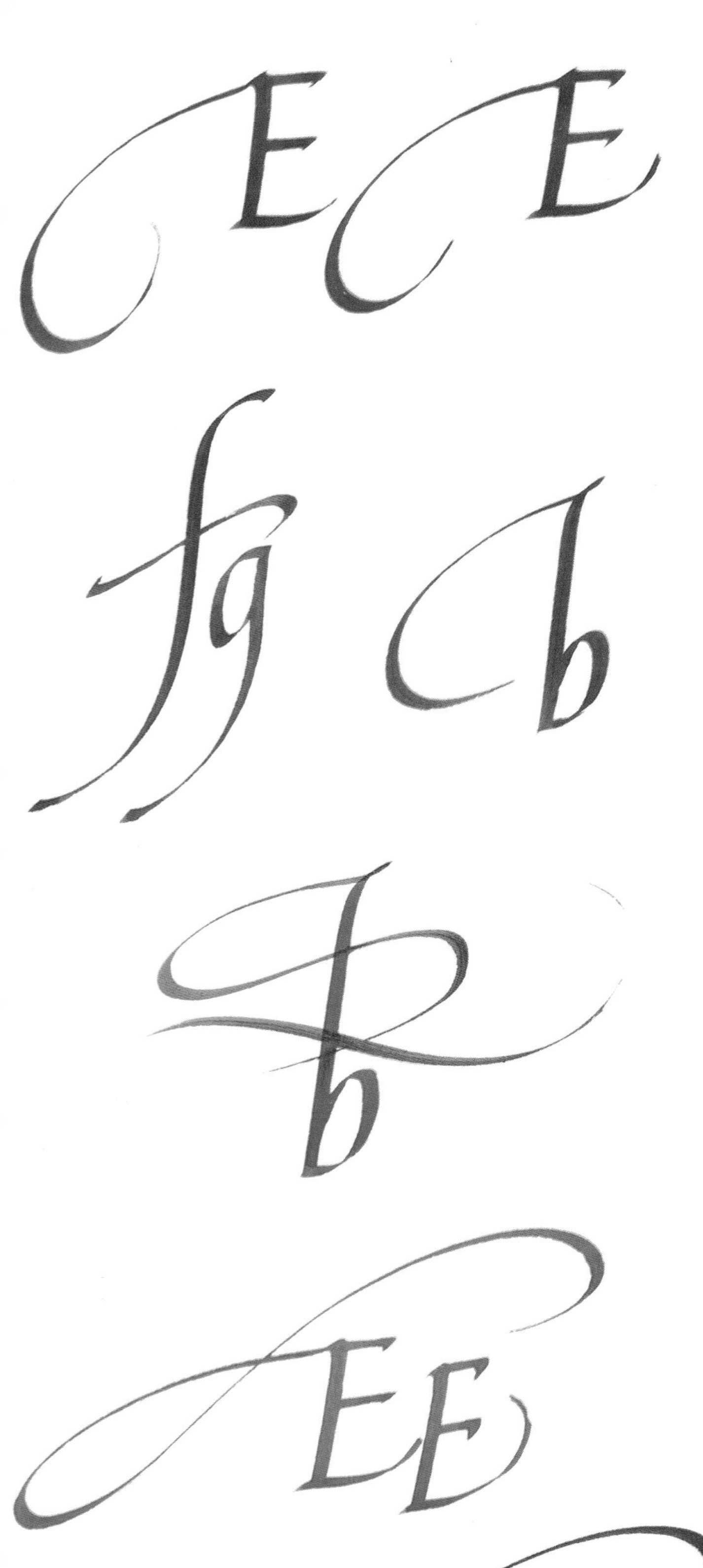

The experiments with the Foundational hand which you did earlier showed that lightweight round letters can look a little too lightweight and airy to be easy to read. The eye instinctively tries to correct this by bringing the marks closer together and making the lighter letters more compressed and oval. It is trying to cut out some of the space in order to make the letters stronger, denser and more legible.

Everything about italic writing is logical. A steeper pen angle and oval letters should feel comfortable and easy on the hand. If your hand is not moving easily, check that you haven't unconsciously reverted to holding your pen at the 30° angle you have become accustomed to using.

Now move on to Exercise 2, beginning with the first mark, the first stroke of 'o'. As in Foundational, pull your pen from top to bottom and from left to right and build up the letters with a series of strokes.

Exercise 2

The letters in this group have an oval base on which to stand, so they must look as stable as possible. You will notice that 'i' has already introduced a serif. As you are holding the pen at a steeper angle the serif will probably be sharper than it was for Foundational, but don't let it become spiky. Now try:

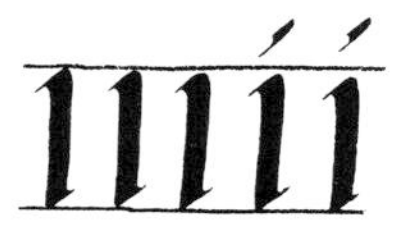

You may find that you can push 'j' to finish the letter in one stroke, but if it's uncomfortable take your pen off the paper and add an extra stroke.

Exercise 3 introduces the next basic mark.

Exercise 3

Notice that this mark, which is the first stroke of 'a', turns quite sharply at the baseline and rises as if it were going straight back up to the top guideline. This is the rhythm of the writing which you were trying to learn in Exercise 1, and it creates the triangular space characteristic of the italic hand. As you are writing, keep thinking about taking your hand back up to the top guideline. The letters in this group have two points on which to stand, giving them a natural stability.

a n

The next basic mark of this hand is a very similar stroke upside down. As you work on Exercise 4, you will notice that several of the letters are made in one continuous movement. If you find this difficult, lift your pen and make two or more strokes. Your hand must feel relaxed and comfortable.

Exercise 4

n h m p p b b

k k r

The diagonal letters are made as for Foundational hand, but should be compressed to give the underlying oval form.

v w x

z y

If you pull all your strokes from top to bottom you will have more control, but you may find with smaller writing that you

Exercise 5

Italic writing has a forward slope, but this is true of most confident, rhythmic writing. Look back at the Ramsey Psalter (page 27). Trying to impose a regular slope is difficult. It is more natural to begin by writing upright and allowing your italic to slope when it is ready.

can make 'v', 'w' and 'z' as one continuous mark.

This leaves only two letters to practise in Exercise 5.

Notice that 's' is made by exactly the same series of strokes as the Foundational 's', but its proportions relate to the oval rather than to the circle.

It is important to practise the letters in their groups so that you become familiar with the basic marks and the pattern of the writing.

Gouache on NOT watercolour paper written with an Automatic pen. Text area 270 x 200mm (10½ x 7¾ in).

PROJECT – PREPARING AN INVITATION

The simplest and most accessible form of reproduction available to calligraphers is the photocopy. A handwritten invitation for a formal occasion, such as a wedding or a special anniversary, probably needs to be reproduced by fine quality printing on good paper or card, but as a calligrapher you are also likely to be asked to prepare more ephemeral printed pieces – Christmas cards, party invitations, change of address notes and so on – which can be photocopied in quantity quite cheaply and which will look perfectly acceptable.

Photocopying is now a sophisticated technique. Black artwork can be printed in a number of different colours; full colour artwork can be reproduced in full colour; the work can be enlarged or reduced in size; and a good print shop will offer you a range of papers and cards in different weights and colours. Some processes are more costly than others, and if you want to print a large number, photocopies can be surprisingly expensive; more traditional forms of printing may prove to be a better investment. It is worth finding out what your local print shop can offer and comparing prices before you make a decision.

Calligraphic artwork for reproduction should be prepared according to a few simple rules.

Page 70. *Two versions of the invitation produced from the same black and white artwork. The original writing was prepared as a paste-up and the size reduced on the photocopier.*

Below. *First trials. The most successful pieces of writing can then be cut out and used in the paste-up.*

B·I·R·T·H·D·A·Y
BA B·A·R·B·E·C·U·E

S S Saturd Saturda Sa Satur Saturday June 25

a a at a at 8pm a a at 8 a a at 8pm

Jonath Jonathan & Sarah invite

RSVP 72 QUEEN'S ROAD RSVP 72 R R RSVP 72 QUEEN'S ROAD
EASTVILLE HAMPSHIRE AB1 2CD

BIR BIRTHDAY B I BIRTHDAY

Jonathan & Sarah
invite you to a
BIRTHDAY
BARBECUE
to be held on
Saturday June 25
at 8pm

RSVP 72 QUEEN'S ROAD
EASTVILLE HAMPSHIRE ABI 2CD

Jonathan & Sarah
invite you to a
BIRTHDAY
BARBECUE
to be held on
Saturday June 25
at 8pm

RSVP 72 QUEEN'S ROAD
EASTVILLE HAMPSHIRE ABI 2CD

Your text must be written in black ink on white paper. A traditional print process will then reproduce your work in any colour you choose, while a photocopy can be made in a limited range of colours.

If you are making a card or invitation which will be sent through the post, it is important to design your work to a proportion which will fit a conventional envelope.

The original may be written at any size with which you feel comfortable, then enlarged or reduced during the reproduction process. The proportions of your design will remain the same whatever the eventual size. However, if you are planning to enlarge or reduce your artwork, check that you are happy with it by photocopying it once before you ask the shop to run off 200 copies. Spacing in particular alters as work is enlarged or reduced and if you are changing the size significantly you may need to adjust your line spacing.

Look again at the photograph of the Bembo sonnets on page 64. At its real, very small, size the letters and lines are beautifully spaced, but in the enlargement the letters seem unusually wide apart. Small writing has certain characteristics which make it work as small writing. Enlarge that small writing and things will look wrong and must be changed if the writing is to work at a larger scale.

When you have written your text, cut it into strips and arrange it into a layout which you feel is attractive and appropriate. Before you stick down your lines of writing, look carefully at your design. In the party invitation, I decided to make the words Birthday Barbecue larger than the rest of the text and the address for the RSVP small and in capital letters. This adds variety and texture to the design, but it would have been perfectly acceptable if all the text had been written in one hand and one size.

Once you have decided on your layout, stick the writing on to firm card or board. It is important to paste your text in straight lines and to get the line spacing even. This method of design is useful when you want to centre your text, which is a difficult thing to do when you are writing freely. It is worth taking pains over this stage: work carefully and be as precise as possible, or the result will not be pleasing.

As a finishing touch, a piece of calligraphic work which has been printed or photocopied looks much more personal and attractive if something can be added by hand. The Christmas card was prepared in black and photocopied in red on to sheets of white paper. I then folded the sheets to make cards and, using gold ink and a mapping pen, added tiny gold stars to each one.

and-a-happy-new-year

WE WISH YOU A MERRY CHRISTMAS
We wish you a merry Christmas
WE WISH YOU A MERRY CHRISTMAS

The artwork for this card was placed very carefully on a sheet of paper. After photocopying, the sheet was folded twice to make a small card.

ITALIC VARIATIONS

Experiment 1

writing

writing

writing

writing

Experiment 2

writing

writing

writing

The formality of a basic italic hand comes from the discipline with which it is written and from the appearance of the writing. If the letters are separate, regular and controlled, the image is one of disciplined order. The version of a formal italic hand which you have been studying is very useful and versatile; it will sit just as happily on a civic address as on an invitation or a Christmas card.

Because it is so versatile, the italic hand lends itself to experimentation. It can be stretched, squeezed, compressed, reduced, lightened, weighted or enlarged and it still good-naturedly produces seemingly endless varieties of useful writing. Once you have learned a formal italic hand, you have a different style of writing for every day of the month, and more, at your fingertips.

Perhaps this is because italic was originally a utilitarian hand devised to be written quickly and read easily and the most important feature of it is rhythm. Provided the rhythm remains and the writing has regularity and flow, the pattern of the letters can be adapted and altered as much as you wish.

For your first experiments with italic you will need a medium-sized nib with which you are comfortable and some pencil guidelines which are five nib-widths apart. My experiments were all written with the same No. 2½ Rexel nib.

Write a short sentence or a long word in formal italic between your guidelines. For Experiment 1, repeat this exercise using the same nib and the same words, but now working between lines which are seven nib-widths apart, then ten and finally 16. You have spent some time encouraging your hand to write even, regular italic letters which are five nib-widths high and it will take time to adjust to these new instructions. Your early attempts will probably look wobbly and erratic, but with practice your hand will begin to feel the pattern of these taller letters and your own styles of writing will evolve.

Remember that writing is always very personal; your writing won't look like my writing and you shouldn't try to copy exactly what I've written. What matters is to follow the principles as

In the morning when I arose the mists
were hanging over the opposite hills
and the tops of the highest hills were
covered with snow. There was a most
lovely combination at the head of
the vale – of the yellow autumnal
hills wrapped in sunshine and over-
hung with partial mists, the green
and yellow trees and the distant
snow topped mountains.

Page 73. *From* The Journals *of Dorothy Wordsworth. Watercolour on handmade Barcham Green paper (no longer being made). An experiment using italic writing at 8 nib-widths high. Text area 170 x 200mm (6½ x 7¾ in).*

Below. *From* The Prelude *by William Wordsworth. Watercolour on handmade Barcham Green paper. An experiment in writing letters 1cm (½ in) high with a small nib which reveals the basic structure of the forms.*

carefully as you can, see what shapes you produce and then try to develop a style of writing which you like and which is something like the examples given.

As the letters gradually grow taller, one of two things will probably happen. You may keep strictly to the formal italic proportions and your letters which are 16 nib-widths high will look very open and weak because there is too much white space contained within them. Alternatively, it is possible that your eye will be uneasy with these large, spacious letters and so will encourage your hand to adjust the proportions. If this happens, your letters will become thinner as they become taller. You will also notice that a tall, thin letter is more comfortable to write than a short, fat letter. The golden rule is always that your eye must like what it sees and your hand must feel comfortable making the marks.

Now, using the same nib and the same words, try stretching your letters, step by step, as far as your hand will allow. As much as 40 or 50 nib-widths high may not be impossible. You will eventually reach a point at which the letters are too elongated to be recognizable and they will no longer hold a pattern, but you may well find that this happens long before your hand gives up.

As letters become taller and more lightweight, the thick and thin strokes become less evident and the writing loses its texture and some of its visual dynamic. It begins to look weak and uninteresting. The balance between the mark of the writing and the space within and around the writing has been disturbed. The same sort of thing will happen if the weight of the letters is increased.

And in the frosty season when th
The cottage windows through
I heeded not the su

Spring

Summer

Return to your original five nib-widths apart guidelines and write your words once more in formal italic before going on to Experiment 2, which tries out some heavyweight italic. Using the same nib, write your words between lines four nib-widths apart, and then three nib-widths apart. Look at what has happened in these two examples. At four nib-widths high the writing is a little heavier and rounder than our basic formal italic, but at three nib-widths high the letters have changed significantly and are almost square; look at the 'n' in particular.

If you keep to the formal italic proportions your letters will become very dense and at three nib-widths high they will probably look quite ugly and difficult to read. However, if you ease the letters a little so that they become wider and rounder, they will not only be legible, they will also be comfortable to both eye and hand.

You will have noticed by now that writing a rather heavy, square italic feels quite different from writing a tall, thin letter. It is just as important to know what the rhythm of your writing feels like as to know what it looks like. Your brain tells your hand what to do, your hand tries to do it and then your eye judges. All three must work together.

It is possible to reduce the height of the letters even further – perhaps to two and a half or two nib-widths high – but legibility is then difficult to maintain because the pattern of the letters becomes the dominating visual feature. This could, of course, be an attractive device in certain contexts. Don't reject ideas just because you cannot immediately see a use for them; they will come into their own sooner or later.

n was set and visible for many a mile

twilight blaz'd

ons: happy time

Having experimented with different weights of letters you will have a clear understanding of the basic letter forms and you should try writing an unweighted letter. For Experiment 3, rule some guidelines 1cm (½in) apart and try writing your words between these guidelines with a small nib such as a Rexel No. 4. This time your writing will have minimal thicks and thins and you will be able to see whether you have mastered the basic form of italic.

You will probably find a larger nib (Rexel No. 1½ or 2) more suitable for Experiment 4, which tries different pen angles. Using guidelines five nib-widths apart and holding your pen at about 40° to the horizontal writing line, write a long word. Now repeat the word holding your pen at a steeper angle, say about 60°. You will probably find that this feels quite comfortable but that the writing is unbalanced because the downstrokes are too light. If you exaggerate the angle still further, the balance between horizontal and vertical strokes is lost and the writing looks very eccentric.

Now repeat the word again, but this time hold your pen as though you were writing Foundational hand, that is at about 30° to the writing line. This time your work will look pleasing, but writing it will probably feel rather uncomfortable. The friction between pen and paper is a little too much to make those branching arches with ease. Try flattening your pen angle further, to about 10°, and feel what happens.

Such an experiment is useful because you can begin to appreciate why the pen is held differently for different hands. Fat, circular Foundational letters feel right written with a fairly flat pen angle, but taller, oval letters flow more comfortably from a steeper pen. With time and experience you can train your hand to do anything, but certain movements will always come more easily than others.

Opposite page. *The last words of Sir Isaac Newton. Gouache on handmade Barcham Green paper. An experiment using italic written with a fairly flat pen angle. The rhythm of italic writing is difficult to achieve with the pen held this way and the writing looks rather stiff and heavy. Reproduced real size.*

Italic letters are oval, but what is an oval? Look it up in the dictionary and you will be told that it comes from the Latin for egg and means egg-shaped. The Foundational hand is based on the circle, which is a pleasingly absolute form, but 'oval' is rather more vague and indefinite. So you can vary the look of your italic in many ways just by redefining your oval.

I do not know
what I may seem
to the world

but as to myself I seem
to have been only like a boy
playing on the seashore
and diverting myself
in now and then finding
a smoother pebble
or prettier shell than ordinary
whilst the great ocean of truth
lay all undiscovered
before me

Experiment with single letters first, remembering that every letter of your alphabet must marry up with your new idea. Now write some words using these ideas.

You can see that many different 'hands' are beginning to emerge from these experiments. Simply by altering one of the basic principles which govern a formal hand, you can create writing which has an individual 'look' on the page.

Take any idea which your experiments have produced and work on it. How are you holding your pen? What weight are your letters? What basic letter shape are you using? Can you create a full alphabet? Can you write words and sentences? What size does your writing need to be? What image does it create on the page? In what contexts might you use it? Any idea must be thought through and practised if it is to become part of your calligraphic vocabulary, but time spent in this way is very profitable.

Formal writing has a natural size. As we have seen, the italic writing in many Renaissance manuscripts is tiny. This still seems to be its most natural size, but it works remarkably well in a wide range of sizes.

For Experiment 5 take any writing instrument which you have – a steel nib, an Automatic or Coit pen, a bamboo or reed pen, a felt marker or a brush – and try writing some words in formal italic at the right scale for each tool. Some cannot produce clean, crisp, formal letters, but they may make a very decorative mark, useful in many informal contexts.

Try your smallest steel nib and your largest pen. Feel what your hand is doing and look at the results carefully. At first you will probably find that both very large and very small writing lose their shape and that your hand is out of control, but with practice your marks will become more regular and disciplined.

Any formal hand can be adapted to create a large number of variations. Any tool can be used to write, provided we are prepared to look at what that tool will do and to use the results wisely. The best way to unlock your ideas is to allow yourself to try anything, and to look carefully at the results of your experiments. Be flexible, but always look and always think about the marks you are producing.

Opposite page. *From* The Journals *of Gerard Manley Hopkins. Watercolour on handmade Barcham Green paper. An experiment to try to create a version of italic which looks cursive and flowing. Text area 220 x 190mm (8¾ x 7½ in).*

Brow of the near hill
glistening with very bright
newly turned sods and a
scarf of vivid green slanting
away beyond the skyline
against which the clouds
shewed the slightest tinge of

Afternoon fine·
Sky sleepy blue

rose or purple·Copses in
grey-red or grey-yellow·
Some oaks out in small leaf·

WORKING WITH COLOUR

Exercise 1

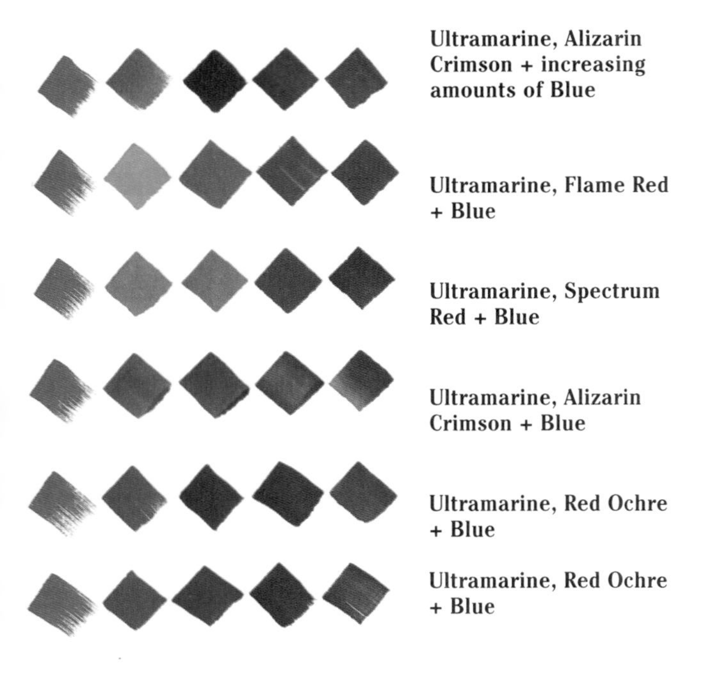

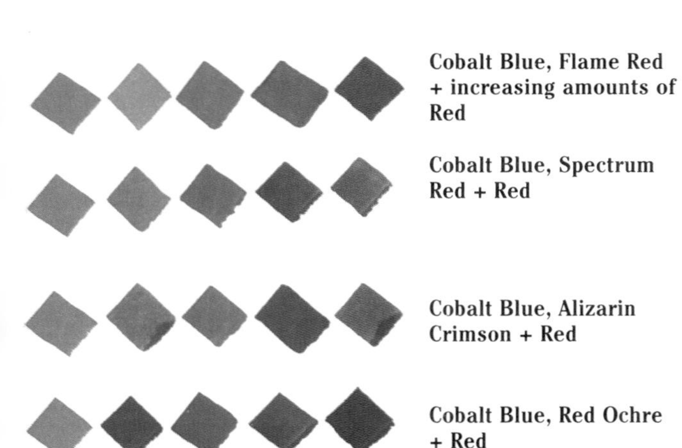

Colour is light. If you wake up in a dark room in the middle of a moonless night your bright red pyjamas are no longer bright red; they only become red when you switch on the light.

Colour is symbolic. In Western Europe we marry in white and attend funerals in black, we associate green with youth, with the spring, with freshness and growth, we use red and dark green at Christmas and see oranges and yellows as summery and warm. Poets have made use of such imagery for centuries, as have painters.

Colour is personal. We wear colours which we enjoy and which we think suit us, avoiding colours which we dislike. When we select wallpaper, curtains, carpets, cars, garden plants, saucepans, colours will influence our decisions and when we walk into someone else's home we respond to colour.

As a calligrapher you will certainly want to experiment with using colour in your writing. If you paint, draw or sketch, you will already be used to working with colours and may well have some knowledge of the physics of light and of colour theory. There are excellent books which cover these subjects in depth if you are interested in pursuing the study, but as a practising artist or craftsman you will probably find exercises useful.

Most calligraphers use artists' watercolours or designers' gouache for their colour work. Watercolour pigments are very finely ground to make them soluble in water and this translucency can be used effectively in calligraphic work. Gouache colours are made from similar pigments mixed with white to make them opaque, and this covering quality makes them particularly suitable for writing.

If you haven't bought paints before, your local art shop will almost certainly present you with a bewildering array of tubes. Keep your range of colours small to start with so that you can learn them well. Choose one strong primary colour such as Flame Red or Ultramarine for your first trials. You will also need a mixing dish, a small brush for mixing, clean water and, ideally, a dropper.

Squeeze about 1cm (½in) of paint into the dish and add one drop of water at a time, mixing thoroughly. The paint will gradually dilute until, when it is the consistency of cream, it will flow in your pen. Feed the dilute paint into a large nib exactly as you did your ink, and try writing with it. If it flows evenly and covers the paper the consistency is right.

If you are already an experienced calligrapher you will probably have a selection of colours in your work box. The primary colours are red, blue and yellow and in theory all colours are made from these. Red and blue make violet, blue and yellow make green, red and yellow make orange – these are known as the secondary colours – but no pigment is a pure colour and it is important to know how the pigments which you are using will behave.

For the first exercise take a tube of red and a tube of blue gouache. Mix a tiny amount of each and paint two marks. Now paint a third mark, mixing the two colours together. Repeat this exercise using different reds if you have them and then using different blues. You will see that red and blue do make violet, but that they also make other colours (see opposite).

For Exercise 2 go back to your first blue and mix it with a yellow. Now try every combination of blue and yellow which your paints offer and look at the resulting greens. This is a useful experiment to do with other members of a class when you can share a wider range of pigments.

All primary colour pigments have a bias towards one of the other primaries. Blues will either be warmer and redder, or cooler and more yellowy, and so on. Three primary pigments will not do everything, but the more you know about the pigments you are using, the more inventive and informed your work will be.

Exercise 3 practises mixing two colours. Take a blue and a yellow and dilute each. Paint a mark with the blue, add a small quantity of the yellow and paint a second mark, add a little more yellow and so on until you have almost reached pure yellow. Finish with a mark of pure yellow.

Exercise 2

Cobalt Blue, Spectrum Yellow + increasing amounts of Yellow

Cobalt Blue, Lemon Yellow + Yellow

Ultramarine, Spectrum Yellow + Yellow

Ultramarine, Lemon Yellow + Yellow

Prussian Blue, Spectrum Yellow + Yellow

Cerulean Blue, Lemon Yellow + Yellow

Prussian Blue, Lemon Yellow + Yellow

Exercise 3

Cerulean Blue mixed through to Lemon Yellow.

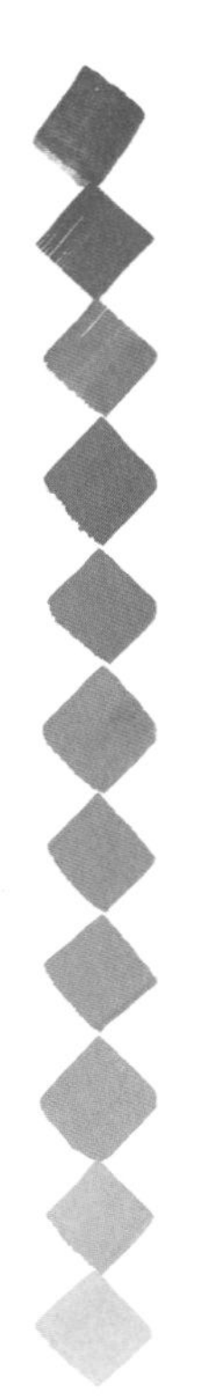

Cobalt Blue with White added drop by drop.

Opposite page. *A random selection of coloured papers. On each, the same green paint, made from Cobalt Blue and Spectrum Yellow, was used in a No. 1 and a No. 4 Rexel nib.*

It is worth combining your other primary colours in this way because you will begin to realize what a wide range of colour can be produced from just a few tubes of gouache.

You will also discover that each pigment has its own character. Some flow easily in the pen, others are a bit sticky or gritty, some are more opaque than others, some separate out in the mixing dish, some mix happily with other colours. If you have tried using white you will have found that it is quite difficult to handle, but because it is so useful, it is worth taking time to learn it. Try making colour strips as you did in Exercise 3 by adding white, drop by drop, to the primary colours to give a full range of tints.

You will have realized that the colour guide on the outside of the tube doesn't look quite like the colour inside the tube; it changes again in the mixing dish and again when painted on paper. The first experiment with colour is to find out what happens when you write with colour. Mix a strong colour in a dish, choose a word and then write that word in every size of nib and pen you possess.

You will notice two important points. One, the colour of the written words is different from the colour in the dish, and two, the colour on the page varies according to the size and weight of the mark. When you are mixing a colour for a piece of writing, you must always try it with the size of nib you intend to use for the finished piece, to see what it looks like. One dish of colour can give a very wide range of coloured marks.

It is also important to try out your colour on the real paper. Most calligraphers work on coloured papers for certain projects and the colour of your paint will change, sometimes to a startling extent, if you change the colour of the paper.

For the second experiment you will need a selection of coloured papers; odd scraps and off-cuts will do. Again, this is a useful experiment to do with a class, as you will probably be able to collect a wider range of samples.

Mix one colour which you are going to test on each paper sample. You will also need a large and a small nib and a few words to write. I made my green by mixing Cobalt Blue and Spectrum Yellow, and I wrote London and New York with a No. 1 nib and Sydney and Paris with a No. 4 nib (right).

First I wrote on a random selection of off-cuts of coloured papers, and then I wrote in green on a selection of green papers. As you can see at the top of page 84, using colour on colour creates a variety of different effects.

Now transfer some of your colour to another dish and lighten it with white for Experiment 3. Using just your large pen, write one word in the darker colour and one in the lighter on each paper sample.

The colour changes between the tube and the mixing dish, it varies according to the nature of the mark you are making and it varies according to the surface on which you are writing. If your piece of work is to be written in colour, it is important to start working in colour quite early in your planning and to use the 'proper' paper for some of your trials. Even white paper varies from manufacturer to manufacturer and this will affect the appearance of your calligraphy.

And of course there are other factors to be considered, such as where the finished work is going to be displayed. Colour is light and natural light changes all the time. Colours are changed by artificial light, by strong sunlight, by grey winter light, by being placed next to bright, colourful objects or in dark corners, by being hung on dark blue or on clean white walls. The permutations are endless.

As you have seen, the range of colours to be made from just a limited number of pigments is infinite. The choice may seem to be overwhelming, so your decisions must always take into account what is appropriate to the final piece of work. Colour is emotional and it conveys powerful and emotional images, but calligraphy adds the dimension of words with the importance of their meaning and the power of letter images. The calligraphic interpretation of the words should always include a choice of colours made after careful consideration of the text and the purpose for which it is being written.

Experiment 2

Experiment 3

Above. *The same green paint used on a selection of green papers.*
Right. *'DARK' was written in the same green gouache, 'LIGHT' written in the green mixed with white gouache.*

Sometimes your decision will be made after serious intellectual reasoning, sometimes it will be much more intuitive – that poem just has to be in green – but it must always be deliberate. *A Small Dragon* is the title of a poem which I originally wrote out as a gift for my young nephew. Rather than draw or paint a dragon, I wanted to make the letters look dragonish, so I started by experimenting with letter shapes. Dragons suggest aggression, which is why the pointed, spiky letters evolved. The dragon's tail developed slowly with a lot of experimenting; the spines on the letters were drawn out with the corner of the nib and the idea came from the natural movement of the stroke and the hand.

I wanted the colours to be dragonish too. I think of dragons as green, but also as red, yellow and orange, so I wanted the letters to be a mixture of colours. After a good deal of unsuccessful and messy experimentation, I made these letters by writing first in a very watery green and then by dropping in the other colours with a brush. I am satisfied that the result looks appropriately dragonish.

Below. *The final title for the poem. Written in gouache on HP watercolour paper with an Automatic pen. The words are about 500 mm (19½ in) long.*

Two books, both using the same text written in the same style at the same scale and to the same book design, were written out by me and then bound by a bookbinder friend, Gillian Chipperfield. We made two versions of the same book because we wanted to compare the effects of using different colour schemes. (Only one is illustrated here.)

Gillian, who makes beautiful marbled papers, wanted to try to illustrate the seasonal imagery of the poem with her papers. This makes a complicated colour sequence on one side of the concertina, so I decided that my interpretation of the text, which is a translation of a long poem about letters and typography, had to use a fairly neutral colour in order to achieve an aesthetic balance. I chose a grey-blue which felt appropriate to the text and was strong enough to sit well against the marbled papers without competing with them. This is the version which appears here.

For the second book Gillian used a traditional Japanese *suminagashi* technique which creates very subtle patterns in black and greys. This time I chose a strong red for the text, which I felt went well with the Japanese feeling of the marbled decoration – Japanese calligraphy is always in black or red – and again created a unified book. Our response to colour is very personal; ultimately we must make our choices according to what we feel is appropriate and what we like.

The book is protected by an envelope made from heavy watercolour paper, decorated with a strip of marbled paper and secured with linen ties.
140 x 300 x 30mm (5½ x 11¾ x 1¼ in).

Right. *A double-page spread from the book. Text in gouache and watercolour, written with steel nibs on HP Saunders Waterford paper. Page size 140 x 300mm (5½ x 11¾ in).*

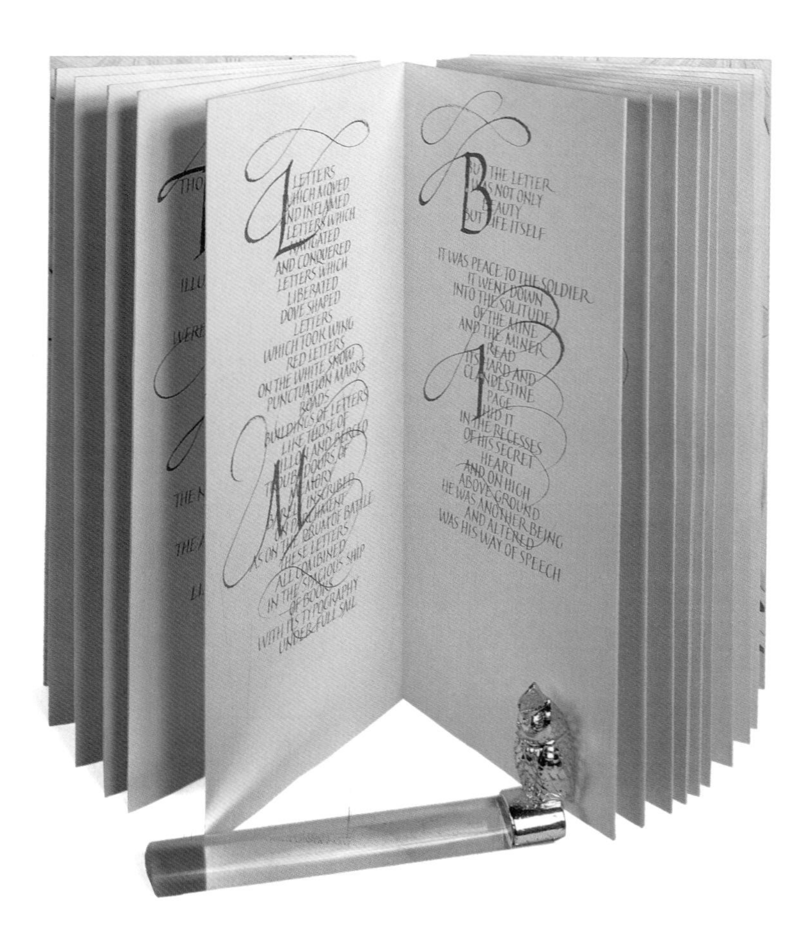

Below. *The reverse of the book showing papers hand-marbled by Gillian Chipperfield, who bound the book. The text for the covers was written on watercolour paper and then bound so that it showed through the vellum binding.*

DESIGN: WHERE TO BEGIN

The calligrapher designs with words, painting a picture using writing, and some of the principles which are useful to an artist working in any two-dimensional medium will also be relevant to you.

A piece of calligraphic work needs a focal point, it needs variety and balance, space as well as movement, and it must communicate with the viewer. When we look at a piece of calligraphic work we need to know what to look at first and how to find our way round the work, and we need a sense of why it was made. Just as the artist wants to communicate with the viewer, so we the viewers are anxiously looking for clues to help us to respond to and 'understand' a piece of artwork.

These ideas are important whether you are designing a wonderfully exotic and inventive panel to hang on someone's wall or a poster advertising the church jumble sale. Before you can begin to design, you must know what meaning or feeling you are hoping to convey and what is the purpose of this piece of writing. It may be to practise italic writing, to congratulate a friend, to express your understanding of T.S. Eliot's poetry or to learn to use blue. If you can clarify your intentions, many of the design decisions will make themselves.

An invitation gives information, so it must be easy to read. A formal italic hand printed in a centred layout on gold-edged white card would be appropriate for Jane and Michael's rather grand wedding, whereas Dora and Stan's golden wedding party at the local pub might have a much more freely written invitation photocopied on to bright card. Each invitation is equally appropriate to its task of giving a flavour of the proposed event, but each must be legible and clearly organized if it is to do the job properly.

A poster also gives information, but it has an additional purpose – to persuade. For the first experiment, work quickly with a large pen or felt-tip. Take the words shown in artwork a), on the right, and write them as a list using the same hand in the same size all the way through. Repeat the exercise, but this time write all but the words 'Jumble Sale' in a smaller size, as shown in artwork b), overleaf. Now write your list for

Experiment 1

a)

JUMBLE SALE
CHURCH HALL
SATURDAY APRIL 2
ADMISSION 20p
PROFITS TO THE
ORGAN FUND

b)

c)

JUMBLE SALE

CHURCH HALL
SATURDAY
APRIL 2

ADMISSION 20p
PROFITS TO THE
ORGAN FUND

a third time, using the two different sizes of writing but introducing space between the large and small text, as in artwork c), below.

Pin your three pieces of paper on the wall and stand as far back as you can.

You will notice that all three versions are legible, but at different distances. b) and c) have the advantage of catching the eye and if the viewer is interested in jumble sales, he will be drawn closer to read the smaller text. c) has introduced space and makes a more pleasing shape on the page. The different sizes and the space are making the poster both more legible and more attractive.

The calligrapher is often doing the same job as an actor. To persuade the audience to listen to, and to understand, his words, the actor will sometimes speak loudly, sometimes quietly, he will vary the pace of his speech and use pauses so that silence becomes just as important as the sound of his voice. The variety in his voice will help him to hold the interest of the audience and to communicate his meaning. Your posters are doing the same thing visually. a) is spoken in a monotone and, although it looks pleasant, the viewer must work quite hard to read and understand it. b) varies the volume and tells the viewer the most important information in a loud voice, but c) has thought about breathing spaces and pauses, so that the poster not only looks more attractive, it also helps the reader to absorb the information.

If you go on experimenting quickly with felt-tips, you will find that other ideas come to you quite easily.

Just as letters and writing are patterns, shapes and spaces, so calligraphic design is also about marks and spaces, about making patterns on the page. That we are concerned with text and meaning adds a very significant dimension to our work and we must always be conscious of the words, of what they say and of how we interpret that meaning visually. However, it is also important for us to be aware of the preconceptions we have about writing which may be limiting our visual ideas.

In many cultures, including the Western tradition, people usually write from left to right in straight lines beginning in the top left-hand corner. They try to be neat and they will probably apologize for their handwriting if they know they are talking to a calligrapher. Ask Westerners to write an alphabet and they will begin at A and go through to Z.

Why? Because most of these actions are part of the way we've thought about writing all our lives and are essential to literacy. As calligraphers we may wish to keep to these 'rules', but we are also working visually and if we are aware of these preconceptions we can use them creatively.

For the second experiment we are removing the dimension of words and just thinking visually. Take some dark coloured paper and cut six strips, each 3cm x 12cm (1in x 4in). On a sheet of white layout paper, arrange your strips in a pattern which holds together. See a) to d).

Experiment 2

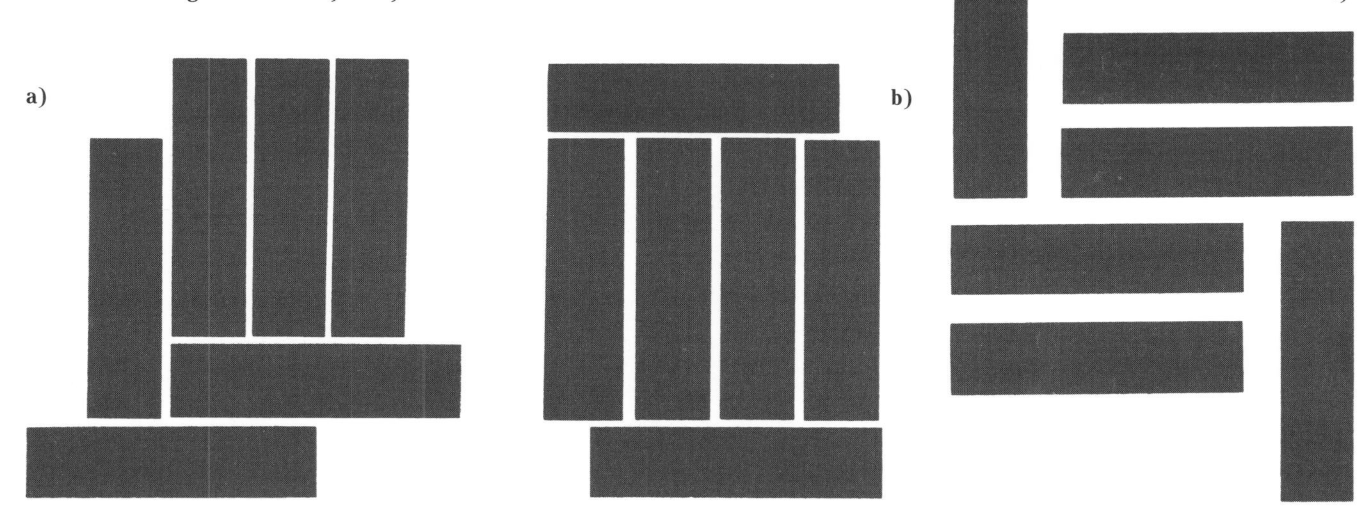

Some of these patterns are more satisfying than others because of the shapes made by the coloured strips and because of the white spaces which have been created. Try turning the page through 90° and then 180° – which is the top of each pattern? The white channels in c) are much wider than those in b) – which do you find the more pleasing? A calligraphic design will need a similar sense of pattern and structure.

Next cut four more strips, each 3cm x 6cm (1in x 2in), and arrange all ten strips into a cohesive pattern. You will probably find that this takes longer. See e) to g).

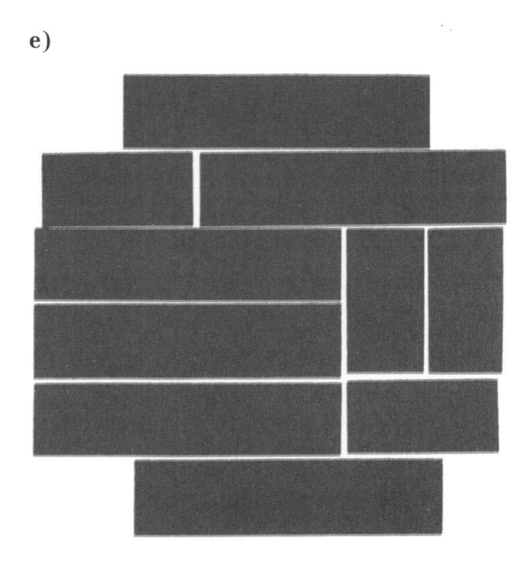

Imagine putting a frame around patterns e), f) and g), and look at the white spaces which now become part of each design. If you think of the coloured strips as lines or blocks of writing, the white channels and spaces will also be a part of your design. Look at Experiment 5 (page 92), which makes the same point.

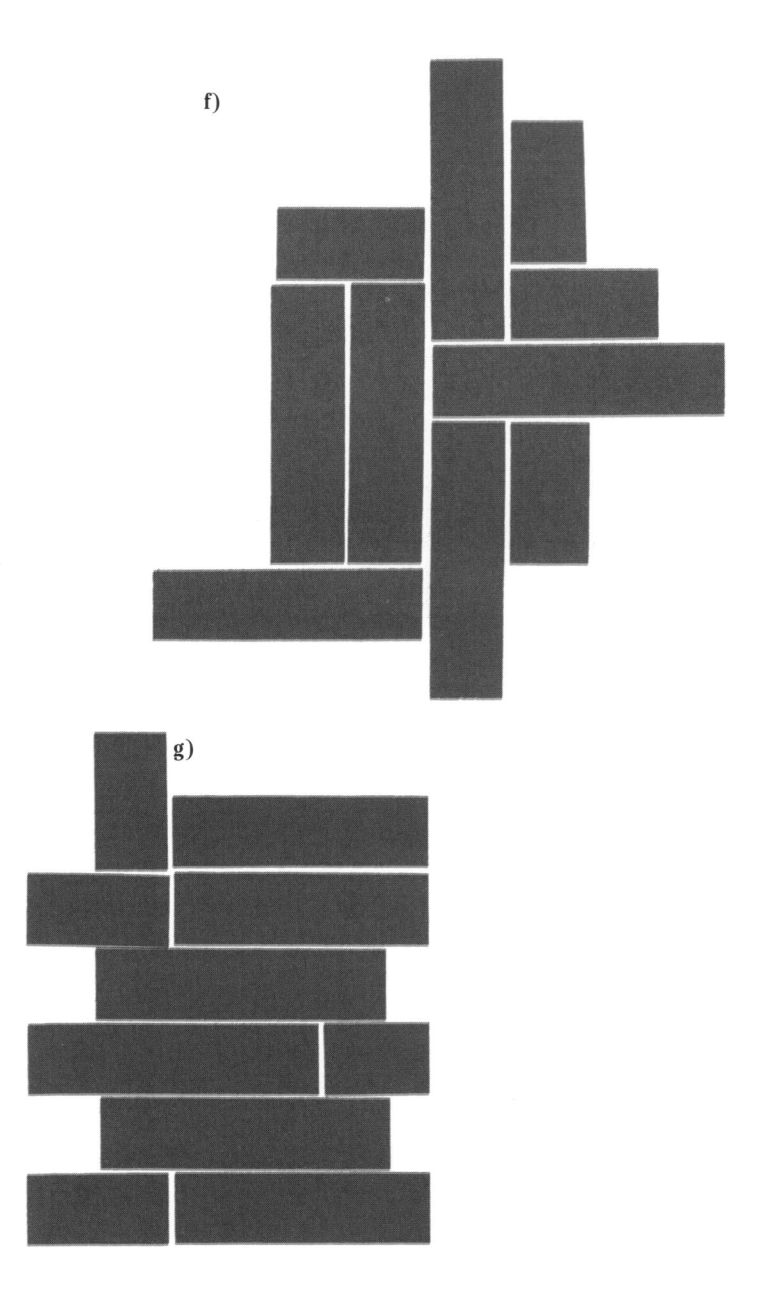

Now cut a piece of bright red paper to 3cm x 3cm (1in x 1in), and make a pattern using all eleven pieces of paper. Walk round your pattern and look at it from all angles. Where is the top? That little red square is very powerful. It creates all kinds of problems and must be handled sensitively, but it brings the pattern to life. It becomes a focal point because it is different, just like the initial capitals the medieval scribe enlarged, coloured and decorated, or the words 'Jumble Sale' which the modern calligrapher decides should be larger than the rest of the text on a poster.

h)

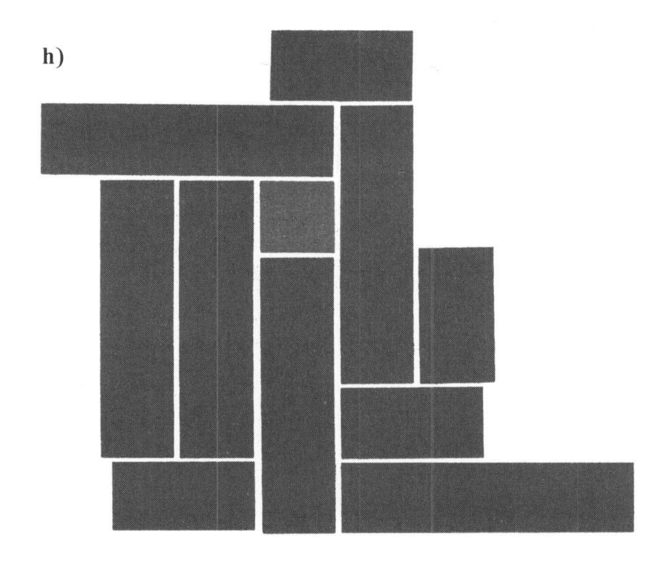

i)

Any piece of calligraphy needs a focal point. Try looking at h) and i) from different angles – where is the top? And where is the frame? Which of the patterns do you find the more comfortable?

For the third experiment, make a list of any seven words which you like. I've chosen the word 'butterfly' in seven different languages. You are now going to repeat Exercise 2 using real words, but with no meaning to consider.

Using a large pen and any colour which you enjoy, write out your words in capital letters, all the same height, weight and colour. Cut out each word and make a pattern on a sheet of layout paper as you did with the coloured strips.

Experiment 3

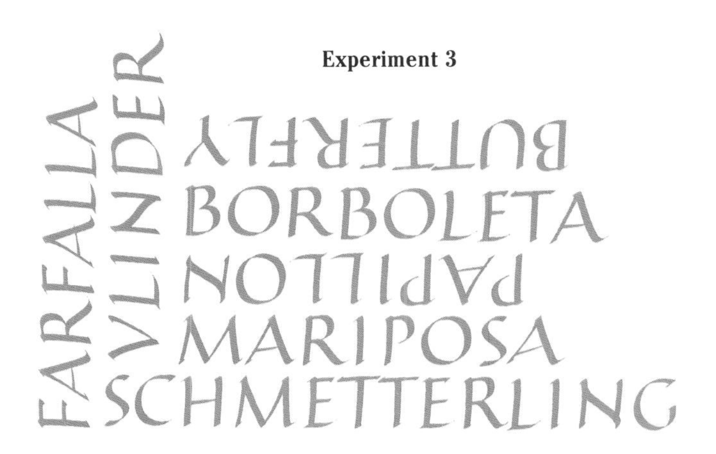

Left and page 92. *I am not suggesting that writing upside down is an essential element of calligraphic design. What matters is that you assess the visual effects of what you are writing on the page. Are you assuming that you must write in straight lines from left to right? Are you really looking at what you are doing? Must you begin in the top left-hand corner?*

SCHMETTERLING
BUTTERFLY MARIPOSA
BORBOLETA
FARFALLA VLINDER
PAPILLON

Now, for Experiment 4, try the same exercise, but using lower case letters written with the same large pen.

Although these pieces of work have no meaning, just using real words introduces new ideas. You may be worried about not being able to read them easily or about words being upside down; and you will find that the pattern written in minuscules is much more complicated because you have ascenders and descenders to accommodate. However, you have created some interesting shapes on the page which will give you ideas for future designs. If you don't like upside-down text, don't write it that way. The choice is yours, but the more flexibly you allow yourself to experiment, the more ideas will come to you, giving you a much wider calligraphic vocabulary with which to work.

Experiment 5

Remember that the spaces you leave are every bit as important as the marks you make. We are sometimes so occupied with the letters we are writing that we forget that there are spaces between the lines, around and between blocks of writing, between words and around the outside edge of the piece. All these spaces should be pleasing shapes too.

For Experiment 5, cut six more strips of white paper and make patterns with them on a coloured background. Look at the pattern of the white strips, but look also at the shapes you are making with the dark colour.

For Experiment 6, choose any one of your words and write it with your largest pen in any hand you choose. Now look at the spaces you have created around your writing where you might put your other words. You may find it helpful to doodle with felt-tips at this stage. Give yourself time, don't expect things to happen too quickly, and the ideas will begin to come. You will probably reject most of them, but somewhere there will be ideas which you can use in the future.

Opposite page. *The word butterfly was written freely and then other words added to make a word pattern. Many calligraphers make alphabet patterns – why not word patterns? Text area 360 x 280mm (14¼ x 11 in).*

Experiment 6

Your calligraphic experience is building all the time and the design of a piece of work requires that you use all your skills. You must choose the right tools and materials; your style of writing must present the right image for the text; the colours should give the right visual messages; and the scale at which you work must be appropriate. These are all as important to your design as where you decide to make the marks and where you leave the spaces.

If you are not very experienced with calligraphic design, don't make the mistake of trying to be clever and original. Someone else is almost certain to have had exactly the same idea and sometimes it seems that we are all constantly reinventing the wheel. Often the apparently simple centred layout or a design with a straight left edge and a ragged right edge is the most appropriate for the piece of work; for all its simplicity it will look beautiful if you execute it properly.

Curved or diagonal lines are often too eye-catching and can dominate a design, so they must be used with restraint and care; look again at the patterns made with the coloured strips.

A piece of calligraphy must hang together, it must look like a 'thing' on its piece of paper. Look again at the coloured strips. The best patterns hold together as shapes on the page with space around them. There is some internal space which is also a part of the pattern, and in the more interesting designs there is some variety. But remember the little red square; a design needs less variety than you might think to create enough tension for it to be interesting.

The most common design fault in the work of inexperienced calligraphers is that they put too many ideas into a piece of work. When I was discussing patterns and letter shapes I said that we all like patterns because we like order; we also like variety, but not too much of it, because then we feel that we have lost control and are risking chaos. The same is true of design. We like the order of a simply designed panel of writing, we like its regularity, the controlled skill, the mood of calm, but we also enjoy the dynamic of a little irregularity, something to surprise us, to catch us unawares and to make us think. We need some little red squares, but not too many.

PROJECT – A CALLIGRAPHIC T-SHIRT

There are various techniques for printing on fabric. For this T-shirt I used one of the simplest, a colour photocopying system available at certain copy shops which reproduced my artwork directly on to the shirt. This was adequate because I was not expecting immaculate colour reproduction and I wanted only a few printed shirts for friends. A long print run would probably need a silk-screen print process: there are many printers who could offer you that service and who could explain how you should prepare your artwork.

I had to make a number of design decisions before I could produce the artwork. First of all, my design was limited to the dimensions the print system could cope with. As I was going to wear the T-shirt myself, it had to have a message with which I was comfortable and it had to be in a colour scheme which I liked and could wear.

I decided on an alphabet rather than words, as this made a pleasing pattern at the right scale for the shirt. The colour scheme goes with a favourite skirt, uses pigments which behave well together to achieve the effect I wanted and which reproduced very accurately. I deliberately softened the shapes of the capitals and used some flourishes to make them look more friendly and informal.

The photocopying process then reproduced the panel on to a cotton shirt. This is one of only six – a very limited edition.

The artwork for the T-shirt, shown on page 96, fits the dimensions of the reproduction almost exactly. It is important to design a shape which fits the garment but meets the requirements of the reproduction process.

ABCDE
FGHIJK
LMNO
PQRST
UVW
XYZ

CALLIGRAPHIC TEXTURE

Calligraphic design is visual, and the purpose of the experiments in the previous section was to help you to begin to find visual ideas which will be useful in your calligraphic pieces. But calligraphy also uses words, and the additional intellectual and emotional dimensions which they add must always be considered as part of the design process. This is equally relevant whether you are designing a label for homemade jam or writing a calligraphic interpretation of great poetry; your work should look good, be true to the words and be appropriate for its purpose.

Writing is usually linear and although we can experiment with other visual presentations of words and text, we usually write in straight lines.

Panel of texts about music, written in gouache on HP watercolour paper with steel nibs. Text area 500 x 370 mm (19¾ x 14½ in). Look back at the experiments on pages 89–92 to see some of their relevance.

MUSIC
IS A THING
WHICH
DELIGHTETH
ALL AGES
AND
BESEEMETH
ALL STATES
A THING
AS
SEASONABLE
IN GRIEF
AS IN
JOY

MUSIC THE FIERCEST GRIEF CAN CHARM
AND FATE'S SEVEREST RAGE DISARM
MUSIC CAN SOFTEN PAIN TO EASE
AND MAKE DESPAIR AND MADNESS PLEASE
OUR JOYS BELOW IT CAN IMPROVE
AND ANTEDATE THE BLISS ABOVE

ALL MUSIC
IS WHAT AWAKES
FROM YOU WHEN
YOU ARE REMINDED
BY THE INSTRUMENTS
IT IS NOT THE VIOLINS
AND THE CORNETS
IT IS NOT THE OBOE OR
THE BEATING DRUMS
NOR THE SCORE OF
THE BARITONE SINGER
SINGING HIS SWEET
ROMANZA NOR THAT
OF THE MEN'S CHORUS
NOR THAT OF THE
WOMEN'S CHORUS
IT IS NEARER AND
FARTHER THAN THEY

THANNE SHEWEDE HE HYM
THE LITTEL ERTHE THAT HERE IS
AT REGARD OF THE HEVENES QUANTITE
AND AFTER SHEWEDE HE HYM THE NYNE SPHERES
AND AFTER THAT THE MELODYE HERDE HE
THAT COMETH OF THILKE SPHERES THRYES THRE
THAT WELLE IS OF MUSIK AND MELODYE
IN THIS WORLD HERE AND CAUSE OF A·R·M·O·N·Y·E

O MAY WE SOON AGAIN RENEW THAT SONG
AND KEEP IN TUNE WITH HEAVEN TIL GOD ERE LONG
TO HIS CELESTIAL CONSORT US UNITE
TO LIVE WITH HIM AND SING
IN ENDLESS MORN OF
LIGHT

MUSIC IS
ESSENTIALLY
USELESS
AS LIFE IS

IN MUSIC
IS TO BE FOUND
THE TRUE TYPE OR MEASURE
OF PERFECTED ART

OF ALL NOISES
I THINK MUSIC
THE LEAST DISAGREEABLE

IN MUSIC
THE DIGNITY OF ART SEEMS TO FIND
SUPREME EXPRESSION

SEE DEEP ENOUGH AND YOU SEE MUSICALLY THE HEART OF NATURE BEING EVERYWHERE MUSIC IF YOU CAN ONLY REACH IT

THE AIR WITH VARIATIONS, A DINNER OF ONE
SORT OF FISH SERVED UP IN MANY COURSES
WITH DIFFERENT COOKING AND SAUCES
IS ONE OF THE VERY EARLIEST
INSTRUMENTAL FORMS

THE MAN THAT HATH NO MUSIC IN HIMSELF
NOR IS NOT MOVED WITH CONCORD OF SWEET SOUNDS
IS FIT FOR TREASONS STRATAGEMS AND SPOILS
THE MOTIONS OF HIS SPIRIT ARE DULL AS NIGHT
AND HIS AFFECTIONS DARK AS EREBUS
LET NO SUCH MAN BE TRUSTED

I have emphasized the importance of spaces. The following experiments are concerned with lines of writing and the spaces between and around them. Before you can try Experiment 1, you will need a piece of text to copy – about 40 words will be plenty – and a medium-sized nib. Rule some writing guidelines four nib-widths apart and about 18cm (7in) long with an eight nib-widths space between each pair of lines. Write out about six lines of your text in Foundational hand so that you are creating a block 18 cm (7in) wide. Then write out the six lines again, but this time increase the space between the lines of writing to ten nib-widths. Now write out the same six lines again, but decrease the space between the writing lines, first to six nib-widths and then to four. Pin your four pieces of text on the wall and stand back.

You will see that by varying the size of the spaces, you have significantly altered the look of your writing and have created different textures on the page. All of these will be useful in different contexts. Keep a note of which you think is the most legible at a distance, which close to, which the most dramatic, which the most formal and so on.

The second experiment is a variation on this. Again rule some guidelines four nib-widths apart but this time only 8cm (3in) long. Write six lines of text with the same four different interlinear spaces – four, six, eight and ten nib-widths apart. Pin your pieces up beside Experiment 1 and assess them. You will find that the narrow block of text gives different textures and that you may make different decisions this time about what you've written. The internal spaces have stayed the same, but because the lines are shorter, all the visual balances have altered.

These are interesting experiments to try out with others in a class, because each of you can do something different. Try lines of writing two nib-widths apart or with no interlinear space at all; try the same experiments using italic or capital letters, using much larger or smaller nibs or using colours. What you will discover is that there is no rule for how much space is needed between lines of writing. The hand in which you are writing, the length of line, the scale at which you are working and the colour you are using all affect the texture of the lines on the page, so you must make your decision according to the context in which you are working.

Opposite page. *Early experiments for a panel, showing different textures created by line spacings and weights of letter.*

WHAT GREATER DELIGHT IS THERE
THAN TO BEHOLD THE EARTH
APPARELLED WITH FLOWERS MW
AS AN EMBROIDERED ROBE

WHAT·GREATER·DELIGHT·IS THERE
THAN·TO·BEHOLD·THE·EARTH
APPARELLED·WITH·FLOWERS
AS·AN·EMBROIDERED·ROBE
EMBROIDERED ROOO
OIDE O O OO

WHAT GREATER DELIGHT IS THERE

THAN TO BEHOLD THE EARTH

APPARELLED WITH FLOWERS

AS AN EMBROIDERED ROBE

FUMITORY AGRIMONY AARONS BEARD AROON BEARD ROD
ARRONS ROD CLOUDB CLOUDBERRY BEARD AARONS
AARONS ROD CLO CLOUDBERRYGRIM
ONY

WHAT GREATER DELIGHT IS THER
THAN TO BEHOLD THE EARTH
APPARELLED WITH FLOWERS
AS AN EMBROIDERED ROBE

During your earlier studies of formal hands, you spent time learning to space your letters evenly to create a regular textural pattern. Such writing looks controlled and calm and, at its most formal, will not come between the reader and the content of the text. However, there may be times when you wish your writing to be less self-effacing; one way to achieve this is to introduce texture into your letter shapes and spaces.

In some of the earlier experiments with letter shapes you tried squeezing and stretching the formal letters to create new shapes. Similarly, experiments with different weights of letters created a variety of different patterns and textures in the writing. The third experiment is to try to put two ideas together, making some letters narrower and some wider, or perhaps using some lightweight letters mixed with some heavyweight ones.

Choose a few words and experiment with capital letters. You will soon discover which letters can be stretched attractively and, as you doodle, more ideas will come.

Many of your experiments will look ugly and you will reject them at once, but there are sure to be some ideas which you like and will be able to use. It is important to be able to forget the 'rules' when you are just trying out ideas. If you always keep to what you know will work, there is no room for a new idea to come in.

Experiment 3

PROJECT – A CHRISTMAS CARD

The chosen poem uses texture in two ways. The letters are all the same height, but are written with two different sizes of nib, which means that some letters are very light and some quite heavy. When you use texture in this way, remember that you are making a striking pattern of light and dark and that they must balance. The lighter letters, which create visual spaces, should themselves make a pattern.

For this piece, I decided not to rule any guidelines, but to write freely, allowing the letters to move gently against each other. This lack of interlinear space creates a texture rather like a piece of knitting or weaving and makes the reader conscious of the overall 'shape' of the work. The outline round the edge of the words is more obvious, just as if it were a picture.

The writing was done with two different steel nibs and as the letters were of a more or less uniform height this created a textural pattern on the page. The lightweight letters were placed according to the overall pattern of the piece.

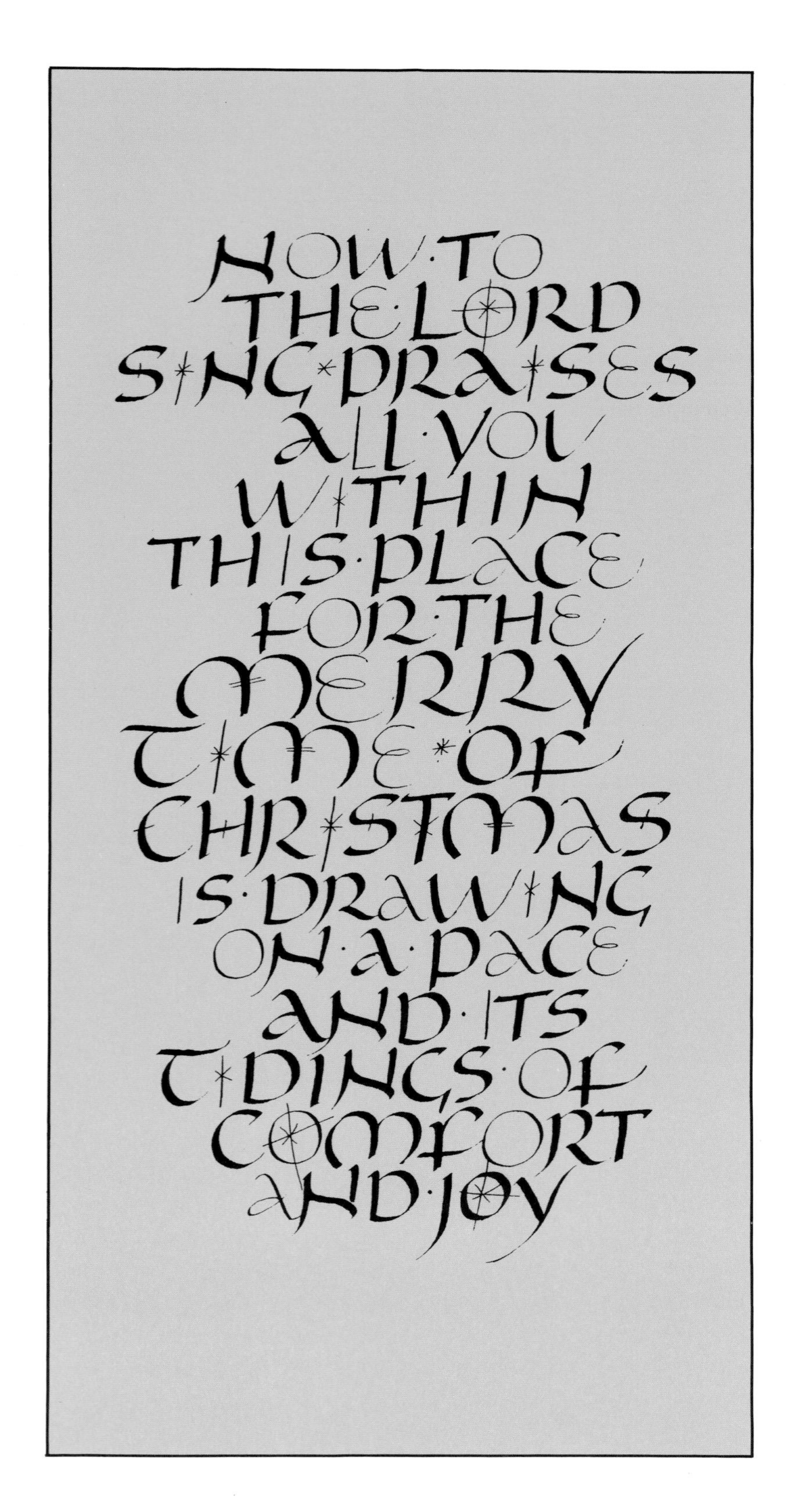

This technique must be used with care; as we've already agreed, such a visual presentation is striking and the reader may be distracted by the image. If your first concern is that the words should be easily read and understood, a design like this is not a good idea. However, there are many circumstances in which a striking image is very important and can take precedence over the legibility of the text.

I chose to turn this piece into a Christmas card. The image was reduced on the photocopier and printed on to coloured paper; I then folded it to make a card. (See left.)

The artwork was produced in black on white and then photocopied on to coloured card to make a Christmas card.

So far you have created a variety of different calligraphic textures by experimenting with letter forms and with spaces. Experiment 4. Try out some of the textures which can be made by using different tools and materials. You will need a piece of rough paper, a piece of NOT watercolour paper, a smooth piece of painting or drawing paper and a large pen such as an Automatic or a Coit pen.

Begin by writing your initials in the same style on each of your pieces of paper. Don't just look at what happens – *feel* what happens too. You will produce three very different marks and you may be disturbed by your apparent lack of control when writing on rough paper, but file the ideas away; they may be useful sometime.

Below and page 104. *These versions of M reproduced real size show that the hand will produce different styles and shapes of letter according to the tools and materials used.*

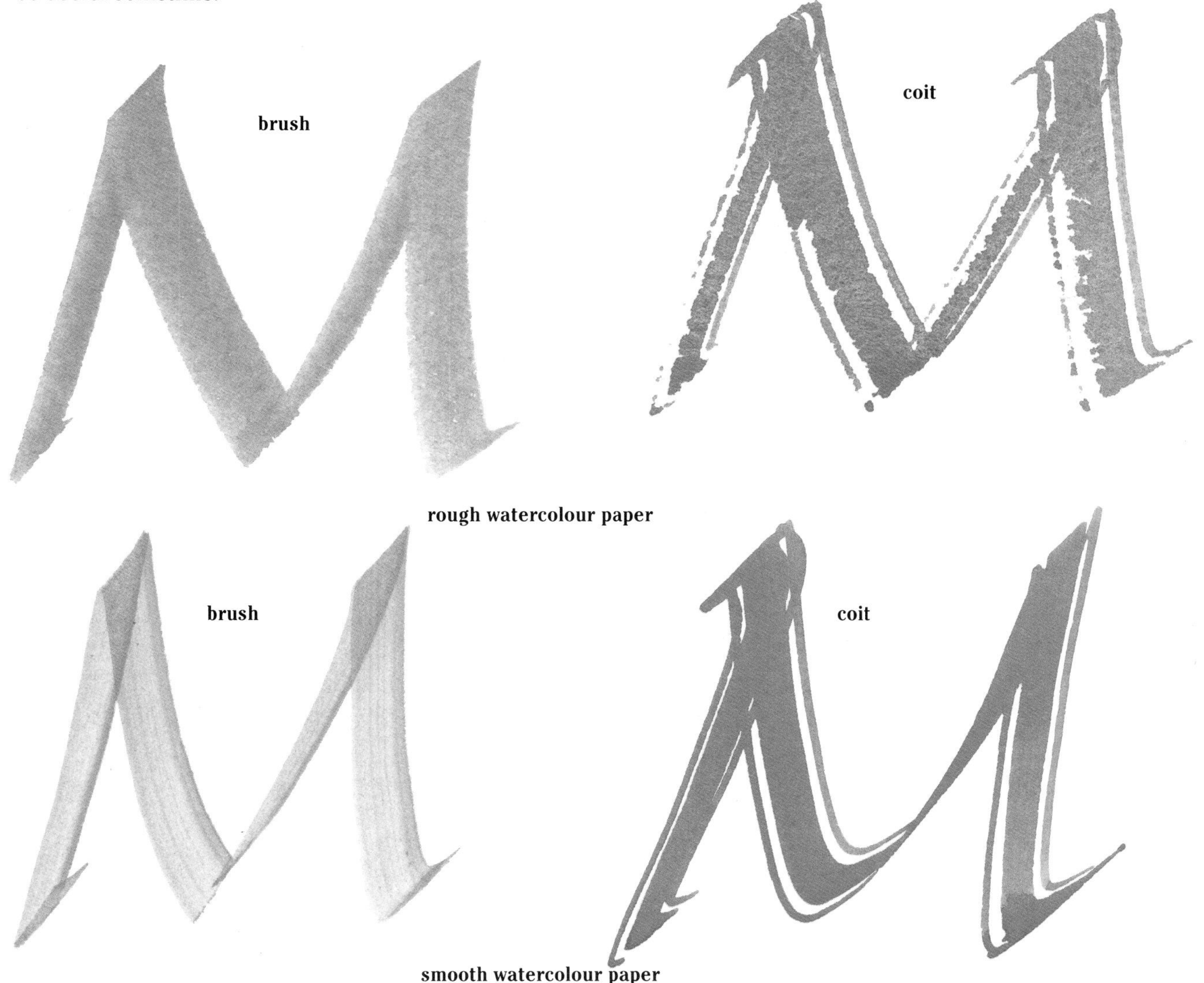

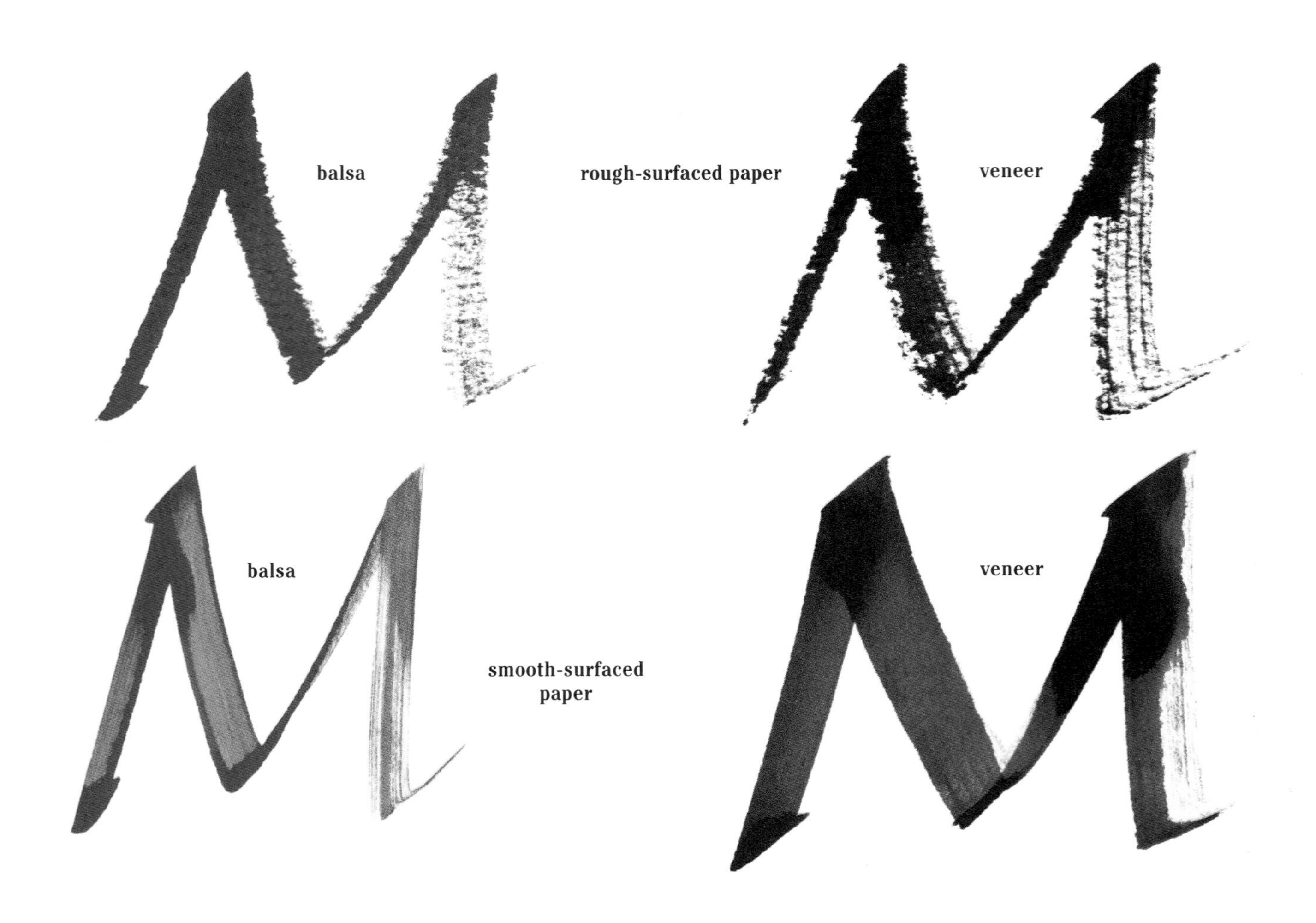

Now try writing on your papers with small nibs, try writing in different styles and try writing with any other writing instruments you have. Strips of balsa wood or veneer, shaped with a craft knife to a sharp wedge, make lovely marks, as do brushes, pieces of sponge and strips of card.

Sometimes the paper creates the texture in the mark, sometimes the writing tool does; often the mark is striking, occasionally it is crude and ugly, but the choices and possibilities seem to be infinite.

Sometimes a mark which appears harsh in black ink will become softer and more pleasing in colour. For Experiment 5 try out some textural colour. You will need dark gouache and white gouache, both prepared for writing; a fairly large nib and a list of words.

Write the first word in your dark colour, then mix in a drop of white and write your second word immediately below the first. Add another drop of white and write the third word below the second and so on. When you have a list of twelve words or so, pin your work up on the wall and stand back. You will find that just by altering the colour step by small step you have created a textural pattern which may give you some ideas for your other work.

The freedom of this letter M grew out of experiments using different tools and papers, allowing the feel of the pen on the paper to influence the movement of the hand and the letter shape.

Now try writing in alternating rows of two different colours; try mixing three different pots of colour and dipping at random from one to the other when your nib is empty; or try putting two colours into the nib at once. You will probably create quite a lot of sludge-coloured marks, but sometimes something you really like will happen. Again, don't try to be too neat and tidy. Many good ideas are the result of happy accidents. Give the accidents a chance to happen.

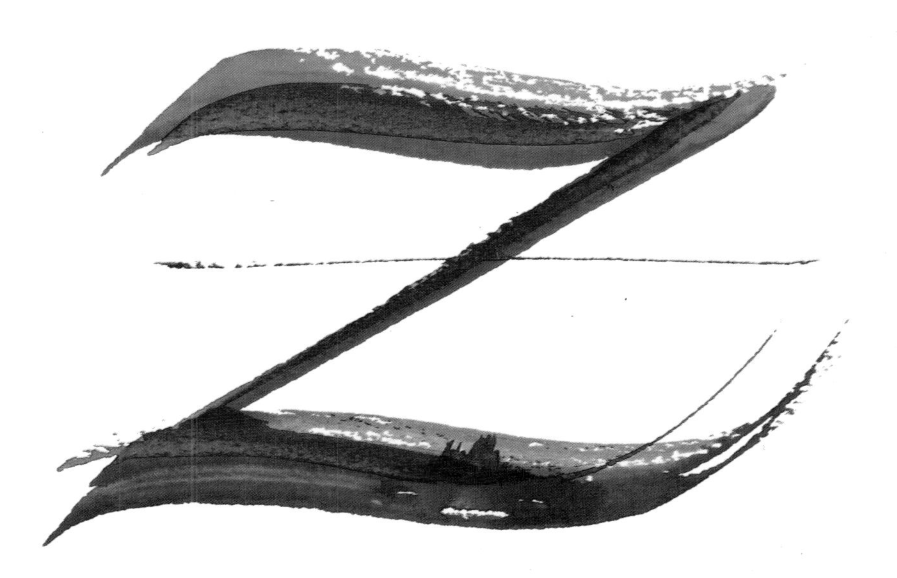

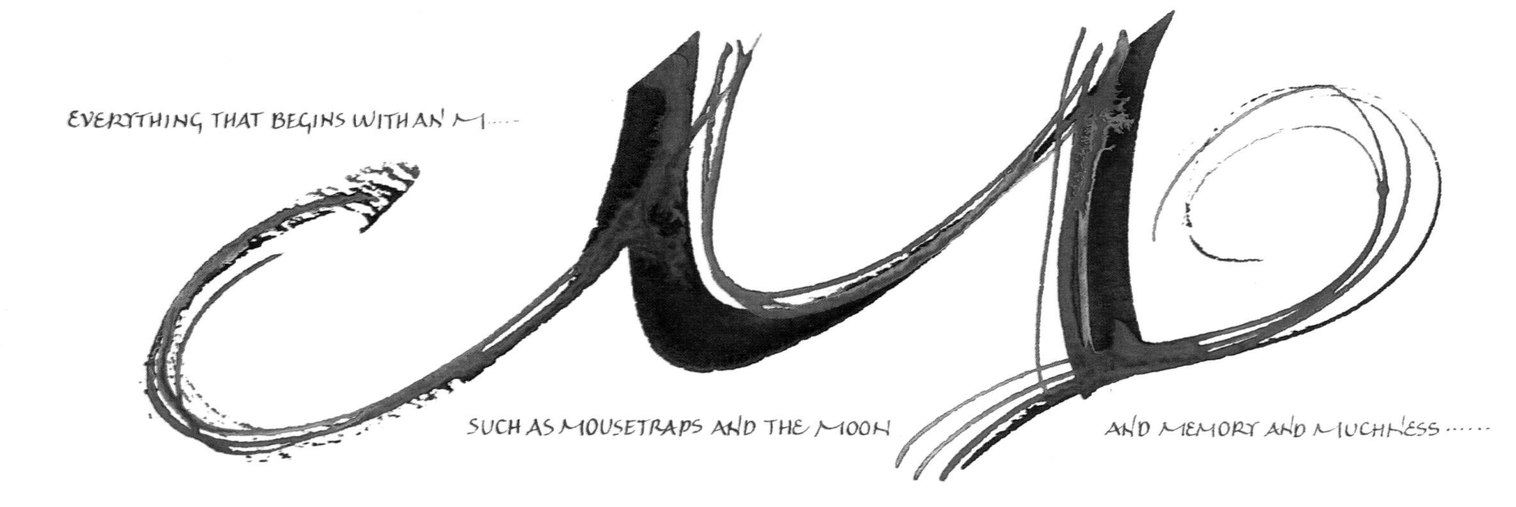

A small piece of finished work and a collection of Christmas cards which grew out of the experiments described.

PROJECT – A GIFT LABEL

A label for a gift can be as modest or as grand as the occasion demands. This was a very large label for a special birthday – I chose this size because I had decided that the message needed to be loud and clear.

First I took the words 'Happy Birthday' and experimented with different lettering and colour schemes. Using a large pen I mixed two, sometimes three, colours in the pen just to see what happened. This technique is rather haphazard and I could never be certain what was going to come out, so I wrote the label several times and chose the one I liked best.

I then added the rest of the message in tiny red letters, cut out the label with a craft knife and attached it, with red ribbon, to an appropriately celebratory bottle.

I was combining three different textural elements in this project. I used a NOT watercolour paper which, being slightly coarse, caused the line of the letters to break up, giving them a soft edge. The colour technique also creates a pleasing texture in the letters, and the large letters, by being compressed, create a contrast with the small letters which have been stretched so that they fill the space.

Label written in gouache on watercolour paper and tied to the bottle with ribbon. 270mm (10½ in) long.

WORKING WITH WORDS

Calligraphers begin by studying letters, by learning to understand and to make good letter forms, and by learning to handle unfamiliar tools and materials. Most calligraphers, however experienced, continue to feel that these skills are never quite good enough and that they need to be worked on and improved.

However, a technical skill is learned so that it can be used, and for us that means turning letters into writing and using words, sentences and ideas. A musician must learn to make good sounds and to play the right notes, but the purpose of practising those skills is to enable him or her to play music. Actors must learn their words, but having done so, they must then rehearse before they can give a performance.

Some calligraphers become so fascinated by the abstract forms of letters that they spend much of their time making works which are simply letters or alphabets, but for most of us, moving on to writing and working with words is an essential dimension of calligraphy.

In the section on design, I emphasized the importance of learning to look at your calligraphy and to think visually about your work. Some inexperienced calligraphers find this very difficult because they have been trained to worry about their letters and haven't enough energy left to think about the other design elements. The quality and nature of the writing is always important, but so too are the other visual aspects of any piece of work. While creating a calligraphic design, you must look at it and assess its pictorial qualities. The composition, the colours, the scale, the shapes, the margins and the frame are all important, but a calligraphic work is a very particular type of picture because it uses writing, and the words and their meaning and character must be treated with sensitivity and thought.

Consideration of the words is usually the starting point for any calligraphic design. Read your text carefully several times before you make any decisions. This may sound obvious, but it is all too easy to slip into patterns of work which you then adopt automatically and without thinking. An evening class student recently complained to me that her work was dull. When we looked at her most recent pieces, the problem became clear. She had used the same hand and the same size of nib in all of them and, although she had enjoyed making the pieces, she was, not surprisingly, bored with the very similar look of the results. The style and the scale of your writing should be appropriate to each piece of work and should be chosen carefully.

Having familiarized yourself with the text, your second step is to decide the purpose of the piece of work. Why are you doing it? What use, if any, is to be made of it? Is it purely decorative, or must it convey information? Who is it for? Do you have a brief to work to? Is it primarily a study exercise? What do you hope to learn from doing it?

It is important to take time to clarify your purposes before you begin to write. That way, some problems are solved before they arise. The scale of a piece of work, for example, often decides itself. A poster is almost always a standard paper size, a card must fit into an envelope, a banner for a church must be large enough for such a space, a letterhead mustn't take up too much room on a sheet of notepaper, and a framed piece, particularly if it is a gift, shouldn't be so large that it becomes an embarrassment to the new owners.

Other decisions can be much harder to make. I usually find that the most difficult one is the choice of writing style. Rather like the actress who needs to get the shoes right before she can attempt the voice and the mannerisms, I feel that deciding on appropriate letter forms can sometimes be a very long process of experimentation, which may be going on all through the design stage. Decisions must be made, but don't set your ideas in concrete too early. A piece of work should always grow organically – so think, make your decisions and then put them into practice, but keep thinking and, as ever, be flexible. If a better (not just a different, but a better) idea comes along, try it.

The first experiment will give you some ideas for choosing your writing style. Using a large, black, felt-tip pen and working freely with no guidelines, write the word 'winter' in as many different ways as you can think of. Don't worry that some of your marks are ugly and that you aren't doing your

Experiment 1

winter

best writing. Now look at your marks and decide which look like winter.

winter

WINTER

WINTER

winter winter

winter

WINTER

WINTER

winter

WINTER winter

WINTER wir ter

I think thin, spiky marks look colder than fat, round ones, but the break-up of the felt-tip pen creates a texture which has a look of snow and frost. Your marks will be different from mine and you will have different ideas. That is fine. There is no right or wrong opinion here. What matters is that you should try for yourself, think for yourself and decide for yourself.

Now take the most wintry of your words and, for Experiment 2, write them with a steel nib and in an appropriate colour. Don't worry if some of your ideas seem to be rather wild; you will find that they have their uses.

Experiment 2

WINTER WINTER WINTER Winter WINTER

The next task is to look at your various doodles and to translate them into something more usable. Looking at my doodles, I think that the taller, thinner letters look cold, so if I wanted 'cold' writing I might choose a lightweight version of a hand, perhaps capitals or italic. Sharp serifs or rather spiky letters might give the right visual message and of course the choice of colour is also crucial. To create the 'broken line' effect, try using a piece of rough paper or NOT paper.

Colour, like scale, is a choice which is sometimes dictated by the nature of the work. If your work is to be printed or photocopied, the cost of colour reproduction will be a consideration. A school or company will probably want their house colour and your uncle may ask for bright orange. A proud father once presented me with a wallpaper sample from his new daughter's bedroom so that I could make her piece of calligraphy co-ordinate.

If the colour choice is completely yours, the decision may be harder to reach, but it will be much more satisfying and again, the words, their meaning and the visual messages you want to convey should guide your choice.

PROJECT – A GIFT FOR A NEW BABY

Below. *'Anne' reproduced at the size at which I decided to work.*

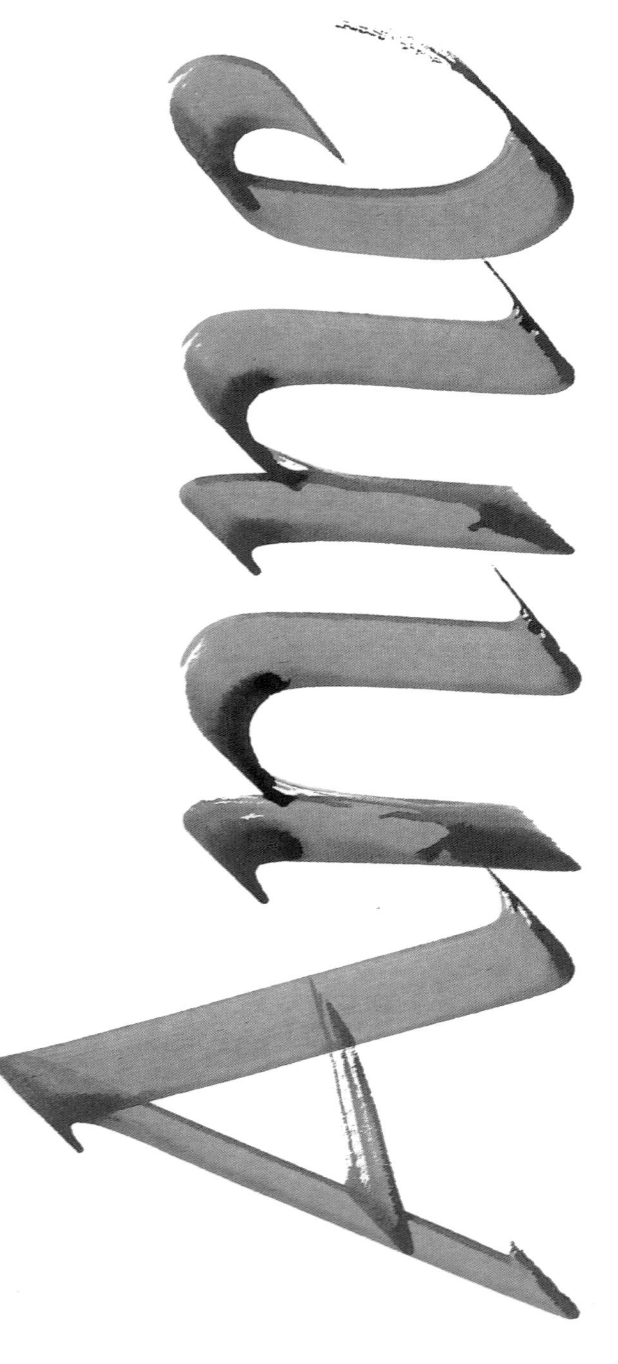

This is a project which could easily be adapted for other occasions. In this instance it began not with the words but with the idea that I would like to make a gift for a new baby. I then had to choose my words and the form which the gift should take.

I decided that the baby's name, Anne, should be the most important element – after all, that was what really interested the new parents. I also decided that I wanted to make a small piece to frame and hang on the wall. This meant that before I picked up a pen I had made a decision about scale, because the name couldn't be too small if it was to be legible from across the room. Knowing that I wanted the name to be the focal point meant I also had some ideas about the design.

Using a large Automatic pen, I began by doodling with colours. I wanted to avoid the traditional pink for a girl, but if Anne were to be blue, what kind of blue? Maybe she should be green or red or a mixture of colours. Working with a large pen means that you can feed several colours into the reservoir at once and some interesting effects result. In the end I decided that Anne should be pink and blue.

It is difficult to make a solid mark with a large, soft pen, so I moved on to a NOT watercolour paper which emphasized the soft texture of the line.

The next stage was a doodle with letter shapes. My instinct said that a small baby needed clear, simple, minuscule shapes, but I did the experiments in case a better idea came up. In fact I was quite pleased with one idea using soft capitals, which I worked through to a finished piece but then discarded. Anne in burgundy capitals was just too sophisticated for a new baby (see page 115). I returned to the pink and blue italics, and added the word 'welcome' and Anne's date of birth.

I then trimmed the work and mounted it on a piece of heavy marbled paper.

Worked at a smaller scale, the same idea could be used for a card to mark any important event, and if worked at the same scale, much more text could be incorporated into the design. It's a very adaptable project.

Some of the early colour and letter experiments. I liked the spiky 'Anne' below, but felt it was inappropriate for a baby.

These experiments are working towards the final idea. Letter shapes and colours are all being resolved.

The finished piece of work, trimmed and mounted on to a coloured backing. Text area 300 x 160mm (11¾ x 6¼ in).

I like the letter shapes and the colour scheme of this piece, but rejected it as too sophisticated for a small baby. However, ideas need never be wasted and this could easily become the starting point for another piece of work.

POETRY

What about working with poetry? At some time most calligraphers will either want to write out a particular piece of poetry or be asked to do so for a friend or relative. Working with poetry does pose particular questions, but many of the calligraphic considerations are the same as for any piece of text. You must still make informed decisions about writing styles, about colour and scale, about presentation, about materials and tools, and about the visual messages which you are trying to convey.

The additional dimension of poetry is that you are using text which is already a piece of art in its own right and some calligraphers find this daunting. For this reason, poetry needs much more pre-writing thought and preparation than most other texts or projects.

Your poem should be chosen with care; it is important to work with poetry which you respect and find satisfying. This is one reason why I sometimes find it difficult to work with poems chosen by others. I like to feel involved with a poem and to have as good an understanding of it as possible.

And that is all any of us can hope to have of a great poem – as good an understanding as possible. A poem is essentially a condensed method of communication. Words and images are chosen with great care and deliberation, not only for their intellectual qualities but also for their emotional and maybe their aural and visual impact. It is this denseness which makes poetry so rich and sometimes so difficult. A reader may well see things which the poet didn't realize were there, just as a poet may think that he or she is making a point which the reader will miss. Communication is an imprecise art.

This is not, of course, licence to put any interpretation you choose upon a complex piece of poetry. Poetry demands integrity. It is important to read, to re-read, to try to understand and to be in sympathy with a poem which you want to write out, but don't expect to find the definitive interpretation. You must decide what you think about the text based on your own reasoning and feelings about it, and design your piece accordingly.

Opposite page. *The framed poem. Written in gouache on Saunders Waterford paper. Decoration from the deckle edges of sheets of handmade Japanese tissue. Mount covered in the same Saunders paper. Frame 300 x 440mm (11¾ x 17¼ in).*

To return to the analogy of the actor, every stage interpretation of Hamlet speaks the same words, yet each one is a little different. Because Hamlet is such a subtle and complex figure, there is room for each actor to find his own understanding and performance. The same applies to the calligrapher's way of interpreting a poem.

PROJECT – INTERPRETING A POEM

When I write out a poem it has often been in my 'things to write' file for a long period. When I came to work on Edward Thomas's poem *Thaw*, it had been in the file for some time and I felt I knew it well and had some ideas about its presentation.

I wanted to write it in capitals because they feel slower than minuscules and the lines of the poem are long, moving quite slowly and steadily. I began by doodling with a pencil, just to get used to writing the words; I discarded several ideas as being too lively, but I soon settled down to working with a particular form and size of letter.

OVER
OOVER
O OVER
THE
THE LAND
FRECKLED WITH SNOW
HALF THAWED D THAWED
SPECULATING ROOKS
SPECULATING ROOKS
SPECULATING ROOKS

The first drafts were made in pencil. These second-stage roughs on the right show experiments with different colour ideas and with different letter weights and shapes.

I have stacked the words into a long, thin shape which breaks the four lines of the poem. I feel that this retains the metre and movement of the poem, but I know that some calligraphers argue that the structure of the poem as the poet wrote it should always be kept. If you feel that way, then follow your own beliefs. There are no rules; you must make up your own mind and keep to your principles.

Another early decision was my choice of colours. The poem is about the end of winter, so I experimented with various blues and greys mixed with a fairly sombre green to suggest the first signs of spring. I began to work in these colours and on good paper at an early stage. The quality of writing changes with the paper, as do the colours of the paints. It is important to rehearse your eventual performance using the real materials.

OVER THE LAND
FRECKLED
WITH SNOW
HALF THAWED
THE
SPECULATING
ROOKS
AT THEIR NESTS
CAWED

THE
SPECULATING
ROOK

THE
SPECULATING
ROOKS

OVER THE LAND
FRECKLED
WITH SNOW
HALF THAWED

OVER THE LAND
FRECKLED

THE
SPECULATING
ROOKS
AT THEIR NESTS
CAWED

THE
SPECULATING
ROOKS
AT THEIR NESTS
CAWED

OVER THE LAND
FRECKLED
WITH SNOW
HALF THAWED

AND SAW
FROM ELM TOPS
DELICATE AS

AND SAW

AND SAW
FROM ELM TOPS
DELICATE AS
FLOWER OF GRASS

THE
SPECULATING
ROOKS
AT THEIR NE

About 95% of the design decisions are made early in the working process. The hard work comes in the last 5%, when the detail has to be resolved. Changes may seem to be minimal, but such decisions are important to the unity of the finished piece of work.

The different sizes and weights of letters grew out of two elements in the poem. The word 'freckled' represented, I thought, a key idea, suggesting the beginnings of the thaw, and this led me to try using different weights of letters to freckle the text. The different sizes of letters follow the rhythm and the pace of the poem – try reading it aloud. Similarly, the spaces are visual pauses, suggested by the breathing spaces which I felt were there in the poem. This is the visual equivalent of the actor's or the musician's pace and dynamic.

Right. *A trial version of the poem written entirely with a small nib was rejected as looking too fragile.*

OVER THE LAND
FRECKLED
WITH SNOW
HALF THAWED

THE
SPECULATING
ROOKS
AT THEIR NESTS
CAWED
AND SAW
FROM ELM TOPS
DELICATE AS
FLOWER OF GRASS

WHAT WE BELOW
COULD NOT SEE

WINTER PASS

Opposite page. *A dress rehearsal for the finished piece. A piece of calligraphy is a performance and every element of the work must be considered and practised before the final version is made. Reproduced real size.*

OVER THE LAND
FRECKLED
WITH SNOW
HALF THAWED

THE
SPECULATING
ROOKS
AT THEIR NESTS
CAWED
AND SAW
FROM ELM TOPS
DELICATE AS
FLOWER OF GRASS

WHAT WE BELOW
COULD NOT SEE

WINTER PASS

Opposite page. *From Richard Jefferies'* Autobiography. *Watercolour on handmade Barcham Green paper. An experiment in writing very lightweight italic; this is 16 nib-widths high. Reproduced real size.*

When I felt that I had taken the work as far as I could, I finished it with a card mount covered in the same paper as I had used for the writing and I added strips from the deckle edges of sheets of handmade Japanese tissues to suggest a landscape. (The finished and framed version appears on page 117).

So what are the rules for writing out a poem? As you can see, not many. The decisions are all up to you, but you must make them thoughtfully and with proper concern for the poem you are borrowing. Perhaps the only rule is always to choose good poetry. A good poem is a complex technical structure and if you are sensitive to its language, its pace and its imagery, many of your design decisions will be inevitable.

The reader will probably be unaware of the deliberation which has gone into every mark in this piece of work, but that doesn't matter. I have been as honest as I can about my reading of the poem and that, I think, is what is important.

Lark singing beautifully
in the still dark and
clouded sky at a quarter
to three o'clock in the
morning · about twenty
minutes afterwards
the first thrush ·
thought I heard distant
cuckoo · not sure ·
and ten minutes after that
the copse by garden
perfectly ringing
with the music

CONCLUSION

At the beginning of this book I said that a calligrapher's first concerns were to acquire a sound technique, to learn to use the tools and materials, to appreciate and to write good letters and to understand what makes a harmonious alphabet. Most calligraphers continue to work at their technical skills, always trying to improve their letter shapes and the fluency of their writing, just as the greatest musician continues to practise scales and exercises. But a technical skill is learned to be used and the experiments and projects which you have been trying have suggested just a few ways of working; there are endless other possibilities. Don't be shy about trying your own ideas. Experiment is about exploring uncertainty, about trying to discover something unknown; many of your ideas will come to nothing, but you will never find out whether or not it works unless you try it.

You now know that there are very few rules and that you, your understanding and taste are responsible for your decisions. Calligraphy is a much more flexible and personal art than you may have realized. If you are to make wise decisions, you must learn to look at and to think about your work. Be self-critical, which means considering what you like about a piece of work just as much as what you don't like. Don't be afraid to make a mess, to try things which you are absolutely sure aren't going to work (they sometimes surprise you), to work simply and directly. You can't help but be original; your work will always look like you however hard you try to hide.

Your opportunities to look at real work by other calligraphers may be limited, but seize them when you can. Join a class. I was very lucky to be taught by some gifted teachers, but I also learned a great deal from my fellow students, just as I continue to learn from my own students now that I am a tutor. Join a society. The Calligraphy and Lettering Arts Society and the Society of Scribes and Illuminators are international societies based in London and there are many other more local groups. Look out for exhibitions and be critical about what you see. Above all, keep writing with a purpose. Stretch your imagination, try new ideas, make things for yourself or as gifts. Calligraphy, like any creative art, is difficult but endlessly rewarding.

THOUGHT WHICH TOOK THE FORM
OF A RUSHING RIVER
WHICH SAILED INTO
THE SEA OF MANKIND
WITH ALL THE LETTERS
OF THE ALPHABET
ILLUMINATING ITS ESTUARY
THE HEART THE EYES
OF MEN
WERE FILLED WITH LETTERS
WITH MESSAGES
WITH WORDS
AND THE FICKLE
OR CONSTANT WIND
CREATED
BOOKS
BOTH MAD
AND SACRED
BENEATH
THE NEW PYRAMIDS OF SCRIPT
THE LETTER
WAS ALIVE
THE ALPHABET BURNED ON
VOWELS
CONSONANTS
LIKE SINUOUS FLOWERS

THE EYES OF PAPER
THOSE WHICH LOOK AT
MEN SEARCHING OUT
THEIR FESTIVALS
HISTORY ROMANCES
EXTENDING
THE ACCUMULATED
TREASURE
AND THEN SUDDENLY
SPREADING OUT
SLOWLY ACQUIRED WISDOM
ON TO THE TABLE
AS IN A GAME OF CARDS
ALL IN THE SECRET HUMUS
OF CENTURIES OF THOUGHT
SONG MEMORY
REVOLUTION
THE BLIND PARABLE
SUDDENLY
BECAME
FERTILE
A GRANARY
OF LETTERS

Double-page spread from the concertina book shown on pages 85–86. The flourished capitals were added with a large pen on top of the body of the text.

INDEX

Page numbers in *italics* refer to captions to illustrations